D0423152

Praise for *Marketing in the Round*

"Dietrich and Livingston have given us a practical guide and checklist for organizations to tear down the organizational silos that stand in the way of getting successful marketing results in a networked media age."

—**Beth Kanter**, coauthor of *Networked Nonprofit*

"Dietrich and Livingston's latest book, *Marketing in the Round*, provides readers with an inspiring view into the pragmatic science of seventeenth-century Japanese martial combat and its keen relevance to the reinvigorated practice of 'Integrated Marketing Communications' (IMC). The authors teach new empathetic and ubiquitous campaign strategies that bring IMC well into the twenty-first century. Comprehensive social and traditional media strategies are delivered 'in the round,' providing practitioners with credible and meaningful tactics, unrestricted by conventional limits of reach and frequency."

—**Mark Meudt**, vice president of communications and marketing for General Dynamics; author of "Supporting Uncle Sam: Ideas for a Unique Integrated Communications Strategy," Northwestern University, Medill School, *Journal of Integrated Marketing Communications*, 2011

"I've been following Gini and Geoff for years, and they are the real deal! In this book, the authors offer an actionable, no-nonsense approach to what it will take on every level to actually communicate and connect with your stakeholders. If you have the stomach for breaking down budget silos, holding yourself accountable to measurable objectives, and embracing a commonsense approach to communication, you'll be the big winners for it."

—**Leo Bottary**, vice president public affairs, Vistage International; adjunct professor, Seton Hall University, Master of Arts in strategic communication and leadership (MASCL) program

"Round up the troops and knock down the silos! Gini Dietrich and Geoff Livingston deliver a practical playbook for leaders who want to solve the challenges and unleash the value of integrated marketing communications to drive bottom-line results."

—**Scott Farrell**, president, Global Corporate Communications

MARKETING
IN THE ROUND

How to Develop an Integrated
Marketing Campaign in the Digital Era

800 East 96th Street,
Indianapolis, Indiana 46240 USA

Marketing in the Round

ISBN-13: 978-07897-4917-8

ISBN-10: 0-7897-4917-3

Library of Congress Cataloging-in-Publication Data

Dietrich, Gini.

  Marketing in the round : how to develop an integrated marketing campaign in the digital era / Gini Dietrich, Geoff Livingston.

    p. cm.

  Includes index.

  ISBN 978-0-7897-4917-8

  1. Marketing. 2. Internet marketing. 3. Social media. 4. Mass media--Technological innovations. I. Livingston, Geoff. II. Title.

  HF5415.D4882 2012

  658.8'72--dc23

                              2012006846

Printed in the United States of America

First Printing: April 2012

Trademarks

Warning and Disclaimer

Bulk Sales

Que Publishing offers excellent discounts on this book when ordered in quantity for bulk purchases or special sales. For more information, please contact

> U.S. Corporate and Government Sales
> 1-800-382-3419
> corpsales@pearsontechgroup.com

For sales outside of the U.S., please contact

> International Sales
> international@pearsoned.com

Editor-in-Chief
Greg Wiegand

Sr. Acquisitions Editor
Katherine Bull

Development Editor
Jennifer Stevens

Managing Editor
Kristy Hart

Project Editor
Betsy Harris

Copy Editor
Cheri Clark

Senior Indexer
Cheryl Lenser

Proofreader
Paula Lowell

Technical Editors
Anna Barcelos
Steve Hall

Publishing Coordinators
Cindy Teeters
Romny French

Book Designer
Anne Jones

Senior Compositor
Gloria Schurick

**Que Biz-Tech
Editorial Board**
Michael Brito
Jason Falls
Rebecca Lieb
Simon Salt
Peter Shankman

CONTENTS AT A GLANCE

TABLE OF CONTENTS

6 The Top-Down Approach   97

7 The Groundswell Approach   113

8   When to Deploy Flanking Techniques   133

About the Authors

Gini Dietrich is founder and CEO of Arment Dietrich, an integrated marketing communication firm, and Spin Sucks Pro, a professional development site for PR and marketing pros. Her blog, Spin Sucks, is on the AdAge top 150 list, as well as being a top 10 online destination for PR and marketing tips, tools, and techniques. An award-winning communicator, she has had clients that include Abbott, Sprint, Ocean Spray, Bayer, BASF, The Catfish Institute, Central Garden & Pet, and Denny's. She speaks internationally on the topics of social media, communication, and integrated marketing.

Geoff Livingston is an award-winning author and marketing strategist who has successfully built two companies. A marketing strategist for 18-plus years, he has had clients that include PayPal, Google, United Way of America, Network Solutions, Verizon Wireless, the American Red Cross, and General Dynamics. In addition to marketing organizations, his strategies have raised more than $2 million for charities using multichannel marketing programs.

Dedication

They say behind every successful woman is a strong and supportive man.
Kelly Dietrich, I love you. —Gini

Thank you, Mom and Dad, for passing on your love of writing. —Geoff

Acknowledgments

Writing your first book is an experience for everyone close to you. My mom didn't say a word as I wrote in the wee early morning hours during the holidays. My dad encouraged me when the days seemed to last forever. My in-laws began introducing me at parties as "our new author." The Arment Dietrich and Spin Sucks teams picked up the slack when I most needed it. And Geoff Livingston. This never would have happened without you pushing me.

—Gini

I'd like to thank my wife and daughter, Caitlin and Soleil, for letting me work late nights and weekends to get my writing done.

—Geoff

We'd also like to say thanks to Jennifer Stevens, Anna Barcelos, and Steve Hall, who told us what we needed to hear. And to the team at Pearson—Katherine Bull, Romny French, and Betsy Harris—thank you for believing in us and our book.

We Want to Hear from You!

As the reader of this book, *you* are our most important critic and commentator. We value your opinion and want to know what we're doing right, what we could do better, what areas you'd like to see us publish in, and any other words of wisdom you're willing to pass our way.

As an editor-in-chief for Que Publishing, I welcome your comments. You can email or write me directly to let me know what you did or didn't like about this book—as well as what we can do to make our books better.

Please note that I cannot help you with technical problems related to the topic of this book. We do have a User Services group, however, where I will forward specific technical questions related to the book.

When you write, please be sure to include this book's title and author, as well as your name, email address, and phone number. I will carefully review your comments and share them with the authors and editors who worked on the book.

Email: feedback@quepublishing.com

Mail: Greg Wiegand
         Editor-in-Chief
         Que Publishing
         800 East 96th Street
         Indianapolis, IN 46240 USA

Reader Services

Visit our website and register this book at quepublishing.com/register for convenient access to PDF versions of the exercises at the end of each chapter and any updates, downloads, or errata that might be available for this book.

Introduction

Nearly ten years since the first corporate blogs launched, social media dominates professional marketing conversations. The effect of social media on the marketing organization is unquestionable. Yet chief marketing officers struggle to define their role within the enterprise. They are the shortest tenured senior executive in most companies, usually lasting only 28 months.[1]

Two recent studies reveal that while the social tools are newsworthy, many marketing organizations still butter their bread with traditional public relations, advertising, and direct marketing. The CMO Council issued a report at the end of 2011, which revealed only 34 percent of its members are completely integrating social media into their larger marketing strategy.[2] An IBM study of 1,700 CMOs revealed only a minority are tracking customer reviews (48 percent) and relevant blog posts (26 percent).[3]

Every contemporary marketing book is dedicated to the topic of social media, whether it be Facebook, return on investment, content, or customer relations. This proliferation of literature acknowledges the change social media brings to marketing. These books fail to realize the full scope of the marketer's challenge, not with social media, but in becoming a modern organization that works across media and tactics to achieve its goals.

That's why we wrote this book, to definitely examine how multichannel marketing works in the twenty-first century in the post-social media era. We realize understanding how to integrate and select diverse tactics, traditional and online—not how to start a branded Twitter account—is the great challenge facing marketers.

Don't get us wrong. We love social media! And we know it is here to stay. Gini is one of the most popular public relations bloggers. Geoff was one of the first prolific social media marketing bloggers to author a book on social media, *Now Is Gone,* in 2007.

But we both have backgrounds in traditional marketing. We actively work with corporate and nonprofit clients who demand more than sandbox experiments without P & L results.

Modern marketing is not a social phenomenon, nor is it an entrenched attitude about twentieth-century marketing fundamentals. This era of recession and tepid recovery demands responsible marketing that weaves every single expenditure—regardless of medium—toward tangible business outcomes and return on investment.

There is no running away from tangible outcomes. Our experiences have been significant in this sense. ROI has been a must whether it was Gini using an integrated marketing and communication program to help a client develop an online $8 million sales channel, or Geoff leading a multichannel direct marketing, PR, advertising, and social media campaign that generated $2 million for the Give to the Max Day Greater Washington fundraiser.

Marketers can no longer isolate one tactic from another. We must break down the silos!

Alone, each tactic can accomplish notable outcomes for your brand. Direct marketing yields the most sales, and public relations best supports industry-wide trends and word of mouth. Social media strengthens customer relationships and cultivates brand loyalty, while advertising brands create buzz. Events provide a platform to execute a diverse group of initiatives with clients, media, and bloggers, and mobile provides a uniquely personal one-to-one experience anywhere, anytime.

Supporting each other, marketing disciplines form a powerful union to meet corporate objectives. This multichannel view realizes the modern media environment as experienced by stakeholders.

Customers—whether they are consumers or B2B—don't consume singular media types. Most people don't go home and visit Facebook for three hours. Nor do they singularly listen to the radio during their commute for information. Reality TV is not their only source of entertainment. Instead, customers consume a wide variety of media, fun and professional alike. This jambalaya of information presents the real challenge for marketers.

How can a brand stand out with so many different messages vying for attention? How can a marketing organization effectively tie together the many disciplines and media out there?

We wrote *Marketing in the Round* to answer these questions. Whether you are a traditional advertising or PR pro, a jack-of-all-trades, or a social media whiz, we know that this book will provide insights into the strategic use of marketing communications disciplines. Inside, you will find methods focused on multichannel integration, a classic strategist's view toward marketing approaches, and information on how to choose tactics to achieve measurable outcomes.

We hope you find the journey worthwhile. If you'd like to learn more, please join us online at www.marketingintheround.com.

Gini and Geoff

Endnotes

1. Mike Linton, "Why Do Chief Marketing Officers Have Such a Short Shelf Life?" *Forbes*, May 19, 2009, www.forbes.com/2009/05/15/cmo-turnover-dilemma-cmo-network-dilemma.html?feed=rss_leadership_cmonetwork.

2. Quintin O'Reilly, "68% of Brands Struggle to Integrate Social Media into Marketing Strategies," *Simply Zesty*, December 24, 2011, www.simplyzesty.com/social-media/68-of-brands-struggle-to-integrate-social-media-into-marketing-strategies/.

3. "The 4 Key Challenges That CMOs Everywhere Are Facing," *Fuel Lines*, October 13, 2011, http://fuelingnewbusiness.com/2011/10/13/ibm-study-the-4-key-challenges-that-cmos-everywhere-are-confronting/.

1

Marketing in the Round

In the late 1990s and early 2000s, integration was all the rage. Integration sought to weave marketing actions together regardless of discipline to achieve a common goal. It assumed that customers receive brand communications through a variety of media and voices.

Marketing, advertising, public relations, direct marketing, Web, and email all worked hard to find homes under one roof to succeed together harmoniously. Figuring out how to add a web address into an ad, direct mail, or news release became a primary discussion point between departments.

We watched companies such as Dell and WPP Group[1] form one marketing agency that worked only on Dell products. They consolidated 800 agencies to regain market share from Hewlett-Packard and to stop turf wars over budgets, campaigns, and results.

Integration was not only good for the business, it was good for the communication disciplines as they worked together to produce results that both built brands and generated sales.

Then the tech bubble burst, and the 9/11 tragedy enveloped the United States, with everyone watching to discover how its horror would touch every corner of the world. The stock market tanked, and everyone retreated to their respective silos to protect their budgets, their jobs, and their turf.

All the companies that worked so hard to break down the communication silos to integrate best business practices lost focus. Budgets were once again allocated by discipline and not by campaign. Professionals were hired based on their discipline skill and not their ability to work with other disciplines. And multiple agencies were hired for one company.

Since all of this happened, the digital and social media revolutions have ensued, seeping into every aspect of business, making the picture even more complex. No longer are companies thinking just about paid (advertising) and earned (public relations) media. They now have to consider the Web and social media and their effects in how we communicate.

Companies and agencies alike have struggled to integrate traditional and social media and to measure results beyond increased awareness and positive sentiment.

People see a mosaic of media throughout their day. Customer brand impressions about products, causes, and services are formed through diverse experiences, media types, and peer conversations.

Rarely is one media moment, positive or negative, strong enough to form a full impression. Before the Web, research showed a person needed to see a message seven times before a purchase decision is made. Today a person needs to see a message upwards of 20 times. Some of those messages can, and should, be delivered by trusted sources, including friends and family, and online friends.

But this isn't a social media or digital revolution book. While companies are quickly adapting social into their marketing programs, it still represents less than 5 percent[2] of their total budget.

You know you need more, but you likely are uncertain about how to divvy up resources between the traditional and the new. The answer is an art, not a science, and it is a result of an interpretive understanding of diverse media, of stakeholders' use of media, and of effective planning.

To develop the art, you have to break down the silos; give up the budget fights, turf wars, control, and holding onto knowledge for perceived power.

The only way to succeed in the future—to best serve your customers, to become an investment in the company's growth—is to market in the round.

Integration and the Marketing Round

According to Wikipedia, integration in the communication disciplines is defined as "the coordination and integration of all marketing communication tools, avenues, functions, and sources within a company into a seamless program that maximizes the [effect] on consumers and other end-users at a minimal cost. This management concept is designed to make all aspects of marketing communication such as advertising, sales promotion, public relations, and direct marketing work together as a unified force, rather than permitting each to work in isolation."

Imagine your organizational structure as a wheel instead of a typical hierarchy. Think of marketing as the hub. The spokes are made up of public relations, advertising, Web, email, social media, corporate communication, search engine optimization, search engine marketing, content, and direct mail. They circle simultaneously.

As the hub, your job is to ensure the following goals are achieved:

- All departments work together, and no single spoke moves into the more comfortable spot of its own silo.
- The days of one-off campaigns disappear forever. No more email campaign one month, a direct mail campaign the following month, a big product release complete with publicity the following month, so on. Your efforts are around either a series or one annual campaign, completely integrating all disciplines.
- Integration is not the same message on every platform, but you're using all communication disciplines appropriately, with the correct messages for each.

- Sales, customer service, engineering/product development, operations, legal, and human resources interact with the marketing round for critical company initiatives.
- Information flows in and out of every discipline in a measured but easy and effective way. Processes are streamlined or removed to ensure that intramarketing and company-wide communications flow naturally.
- You find the fastest path to the end result, with the least expenditure of time and resources.

Are you already doing some of this? Perhaps you're integrating marketing and communication around a webinar series or a trade show. Maybe you're using Chatter inside Salesforce or creating an internal communication instant messaging system with Yammer. It may be that you regularly time your advertising and direct marketing launch to coincide with a major PR announcement. Or you've created an internal blog where all disciplines share information with one another.

Or is your organization so siloed that all you can do every day is protect your own turf by focusing solely on your job and not on what the other disciplines are doing?

Marketing in the round means the silos must disappear. Forever. All the disciplines must work together, no matter what turf wars or comfort boxes your organization holds dear. Sales, customer service, legal, and human resources need to advise and provide input to the marketing round as the situation demands. Those wars and boxes mean that even though you may be doing a good job of integrating marketing, public relations, and email, the other disciplines are being left out.

Breaking Down the Silos

Breaking down the silos isn't going to be easy, especially if that's the way things have always been done. But silos are detrimental to an organization's success, and in the coming years they will be devastating, if not fatal, to your discipline. Things are moving too rapidly for disciplines to be protecting their own turfs.

A siloed organization cannot act quickly, make productive decisions, or be nimble, which all are requirements of marketing in a networked media age. Technology changes the way you do your job nearly daily.

Typically, you see silos in larger organizations, but there also is evidence of their developing fairly rapidly in start-ups and small companies.

According to *Life Science Leader* magazine,[3] silos destroy trust, cut off communication, and foster complacency. What is meant to produce power and control really creates animosity and suspicion.

Just like the corn and wheat silos you see along the side of the road, business silos hold important things and prevent them from being shared with colleagues and peers.

Unlike the agricultural silo that protects grain from bad weather, however, a business silo protects much less than intended. Instead it hoards and controls and hurts.

Do you like hearing about projects that got underway without your knowledge? Do you like not talking to other leaders within your organization? Do you like championing your own cause without support from your peers? How often do you attend an all-staff meeting to discover a new effort you're in charge of executing, and it's the first you've heard of it?

No one likes this. Yet it happens every day, in organizations of every size.

There are two types of silos: the lonely and the functional.

The lonely silo has no connection to the outside world. This typically happens at a start-up, where the focus is on getting things done and out the door, rather than on doing things the right way.

The functional silo has what some may confuse with a team-like feel. There are brainstorm sessions and late nights and pizza brought in, but the "team" doesn't have a seat at the business strategy table. Things don't move quickly, because 10 silos have to sign off on everything, slowing the process and creating an absurd amount of red tape.

Unfortunately, breaking down the silos has to be done before you can market in the round, so you have a big challenge on your hands. You're going to have to get the organization to change.

People don't change because they want to. They change because they're forced to—by customers, by competition, by the economy, by advances in technology, or by government regulations.

You may have to force a crisis.

The first thing you have to do is get buy-in from the corner office. The vision and the messages must be consistently communicated from your leadership team—even if you have to remind your executive team it's time to communicate the vision and drive the messages. They have to come from the corner office.

Then you must gather someone from every discipline. Ask supervisors to elect a person from their departments, or ask people to apply for the positions. This allows you to gauge their interest and level of commitment. Make participation part of their bonus program. Create mandatory meetings where you share data so everyone understands the strengths, the challenges, and the areas for improvement of each department. Build trust among the team.

You're going to be creating change, and people fear change. They fear doing things differently than they have always been done. You'll face resistance. You'll face criticism. Change management is not easy, but you'll be blazing the trail to market in the round, which will make everyone, and the company, more successful.

CEO Communication

Almost more important than breaking down the silos and marketing in the round, however, is getting senior leadership buy-in. Your CEO must consistently communicate the change. If that doesn't happen, it won't matter how well the group is working together; the change won't stick.

Make the CEO's job easy. Provide the messages. Schedule the all-staff meetings. Make sure the CEO is walking around and talking to people in every department once a day.

Communicate every week on how it's going: what's working, what's not working, changes you'd like to make. Keep the vision top-of-mind, and make sure it's being communicated at every meeting, even if it's in a small way.

It's been said it takes six weeks to create a habit. Those six weeks are going to be very painful for you. You'll work really hard. Your CEO will tire of your asking of continually being asked to deliver the vision to all employees. There may even be some animosity.

In the words of Steve Jobs,[4] though, if you know you're right, keep pushing forward and everyone else will eventually join you.

Creating the Marketing Round

After you've created your launch group with someone from every discipline, hold an inaugural, in-person meeting. In-person is vital, especially if you're accustomed to working remotely or from satellite offices. This will build trust more quickly than a video conference or a conference call.

At the first meeting, agree to (at a minimum) biweekly meetings (these can be done with video or conference calls) and get them on everyone's calendars. The mandate must come from the corner office that these are not to be missed except in cases of customer emergency, medical emergency, or long-scheduled vacations.

Encourage group members to communicate with one another outside of meetings—Chatter, Yammer, Skype, Google Hangouts, or even the old stand-by GChat are useful options. Or create a forum, a Google+ or Facebook group, a discussion group, or an internal blog where you interact daily.

Picture a round organizational chart for each discipline, with marketing in the middle, as shown in Figure 1.1.

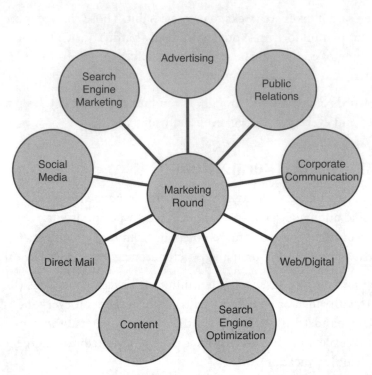

Figure 1.1 *Marketing is in the middle of all the communication disciplines in an organizational chart.*

Communication is the key to all of this. It's imperative you all know what the others are doing, at all times, to make this work:

- Have a new product or service being launched? The first place you should go is the marketing round, to discuss the opportunities and how you can launch it together, instead of in your silos.
- Need to increase sales? Go to the marketing round.
- Want to get customer feedback? Go to the marketing round.
- Need to communicate internal changes? Go to the marketing round.

This is the job of everyone, not just sales or marketing, not the leadership team. Not public relations or corporate communication.

Everyone.

Work together to create the plan. Be rid of the silos.

The Dashboard

In your first two meetings, you must decide on the vision of the marketing round. Then create a dashboard for measuring and reporting results.

The dashboard should follow the SMARTER goals: specific, measurable, attainable, relevant, time-bound, evaluate, and reevaluate.

Evaluate and reevaluate have been added here because, in today's world, you no longer have to wait a full year to analyze results and evaluate the effectiveness of a program. Today you'll know in as little as a week whether something is or isn't working. Constantly evaluating and refining your goals will mean success not only for a program, but also for the marketing round.

Too often we plan, write down our goals, and then stuff them in a drawer and revisit them only when planning for the next year. The marketing round will have a dashboard that follows the goals, is visited daily, and is updated in the biweekly meetings.

The data for each discipline will be integrated into one report, and all successes, challenges, and issues will be visible to everyone. Transparency is a word batted around almost too much today, but trust will not be built without it.

Some companies use green, yellow, and red to determine where the goals stand. Others use a numerical scale. What you use is up to you—but choose a way to show the growth or decline of the goals that is easy to read, easy to define, and easy to fix.

Your dashboard should fit your SMARTER goals and should not be solely about sentiment or awareness. As the marketing round, you should be looking at everything from lead generation and conversion to customer retention and sales.

You also want to include brand awareness, Web site traffic, and thought leadership, but be sure that all of those goals are combined with real, hard numbers, such as leads, conversions, sales, and profit—not just soft feel-good measurements, such as impressions, clicks, sentiment, likes, follows, fan, or plusses. In the end, your marketing round's success will be determined by its ability to successfully impact business, not garner attention.

During a down economy, marketing and the disciplines underneath it are typically the first to go. But marketing in the round allows you to become an investment, rather than an expense. Working together as a team with all members having integral tasks allows the chief financial officer to demonstrate your efforts on the profit side of the P & L. It allows you to maintain, or even increase, your budgets during a recession.

Bringing It All Together

Now that you understand how and why marketing serves as the hub in the round of communication disciplines, how to break down the silos, how to get senior leadership involved, and how to develop the marketing round team and get your vision, goals, and dashboard ready, it's time to begin.

The exercises on the following pages will help you develop your vision, create your goals, and build your dashboard.

In order to break down the silos, develop trust, and gain immediate buy-in, the marketing round should work on this task together. It's not for you to develop in your silo and then impose upon the first meeting.

It may take more than a few meetings to get it right, but it will be worth the time and energy spent later. Soon you'll be on your way to marketing in the round.

Exercises

Developing the Vision

This is the fun, but also more difficult, part. A good majority of marketing professionals mix up strategy and tactics. A tactic is not a strategy, but rather a piece of a strategy. The best way to think about your strategy, or vision, is to think about what things will look like a year from now.

Go back to the "Integration and the Marketing Round" section of this chapter. Is your vision in one of those bullet points? Or is there something else you'd like to achieve?

A vision typically seems out of reach and sometimes overwhelming, but it can be achieved if you're marketing in the round.

Some examples of great vision statements include the following:

- "To develop a perfect search engine" –Google
- "A personal computer in every home running Microsoft software" –Microsoft
- "Change the perception of the PR and marketing industries" –Spin Sucks Pro
- "To make air travel cheaper and more convenient than auto travel" –Southwest Airlines
- "Helping people around the world eat and live better" –Kraft Foods
- "Eradicate sexual abuse forever" –Zacharias Center

Of course, the marketing round vision needs to work in tandem with and complement the organization's vision. If there isn't a clear vision for your company, it's your job to create one and to be sure your senior leaders are communicating it effectively and consistently.

You'll also note, in the previous examples, the vision statements are not long or convoluted. They give people something to work toward, and they make decisions easier by asking the question "Does what we're about to do get us closer to the vision?"

A vision statement has two components: the external vision and the internal vision.

The external vision defines the outcome you want to achieve. The internal vision is one of change, but it also is a clear understanding of the strengths of your colleagues and the assets of the company.

For example, Kraft wants people around the world to eat and live better (external), and their core strengths are providing food that is easy to prepare and healthy for busy families.

As you begin to consider the marketing round vision (or the company vision, if you don't already have one), the following questions should be brought to the first and second group meetings:

1. What are our strengths, as a group and as an organization?

2. What are our weaknesses?

3. What are our opportunities? Where are we stronger than our competition?

4. What are our threats? Where is the competition beating us?

5. Who are our primary customers?

6. Who are our primary influencers?

7. What trends are affecting our business?

8. What trends are affecting our customers?

9. How do we create value for customers?

10. Do we talk about ourselves more than we do about our customers?

11. Do we have anything innovative coming out in the next year? If not, is there anything we can create that provides our customers with something new to stay ahead of the trends?

12. What challenges will we face as we begin to communicate this vision internally? Externally?

Now, write your vision.

_____

_____

_____

Creating the SMARTER Goals

In order to create the dashboard you'll use for reporting every week, you need to create your goals.

In the dashboard exercise, there are some examples you can use, but they are consolidated. Your SMARTER goals need to be clear and use each letter of the acronym.

Let's take sales as an example.

Increase sales by 5 percent in the next 12 months (remember, this is just for the marketing round team, not the entire company).

It's specific, it's measurable, you have to decide whether it's attainable, it's certainly relevant, and it's time-bound. Then you'll evaluate how the marketing round's efforts are affecting sales and reevaluate during every team meeting.

Now it's your turn. For every discipline that makes up your marketing round, each person should create one to three SMARTER goals using Table 1.1 as a template. Remember, they should be specific, measurable, attainable, relevant, time-bound, evaluate, and reevaluate.

Table 1.1   Creating SMARTER Goals

	Goal #1	Goal #2	Goal #3
Marketing			
Advertising			
Public Relations			
Corporate Communication			
Digital/Web			
Social Media			
Search Engine Optimization			
Search Engine Marketing			
Direct Mail			
Email			
Content			

Building the Dashboard

Although there isn't a dashboard system that works the same way for everyone, there are certain metrics everyone should track. Those metrics are listed under the appropriate goal, but they are not, by any means, the only things to be considered for each.

This document, shown in Table 1.2, can be used to help the marketing round determine what should be tracked and who is responsible for reporting to the team. In some cases, you may want to get your chief financial officer involved to help determine the benchmarks from which to measure each month.

Table 1.2 Dashboard Metrics

VISION:

	Responsible	Jan	Feb	Mar	Apr	May	Jun	Jul	Aug	Sep	Oct	Nov	Dec
Goals													
Sales													
• Increase %													
• Sales specific to a product or service (i.e., eBook or inventory selection)													
Lead Nurturing													
• # of down-loads, regis-trations, or subscriptions													

VISION:

	Responsible	Jan	Feb	Mar	Apr	May	Jun	Jul	Aug	Sep	Oct	Nov	Dec
Goals													
Lead Generation													
• # of unique contacts													
Lead Conversion													
• # of unique contacts to become customers													
Customer Retention/ Customer Lifetime Value (CLV)													
• Days, months, years customers remain													
Customer Service													
• Reduction in call volume													

VISION:

Goals	Responsible	Jan	Feb	Mar	Apr	May	Jun	Jul	Aug	Sep	Oct	Nov	Dec
• Improvement in using social platforms with customers													
Brand Awareness													
• Increase in mentions of produce or service online													
Thought Leadership													
• Increase in interviews and guest blog opportunities													
• Increase in speaking engagements													

VISION:

	Responsible	Jan	Feb	Mar	Apr	May	Jun	Jul	Aug	Sep	Oct	Nov	Dec
Goals													
Web Site Traffic													
• Increase in visitors													
• Increase in unique visitors													
Employee Retention													
• Decrease in turnover													
• Increase in morale as de-fined through surveys													
Other goals:													

Endnotes

1. *Dell and WPP Group form marketing agency,*
   www.nytimes.com/2007/12/03/technology/03dell.html.

2. http://www.gtms-inc.com/How-Much-Can-You-Spend-On-
   Social-Media_ep_188.html.

3. *Life Science Leader, as seen in the May 2011 issue of Forbes,*
   www.forbes.com/sites/johnkotter/2011/05/03/breaking-down-
   silos/.

4. http://gigaom.com/2011/08/24/steve-jobs-the-sound-of-silence/.

2

Know All the Tools

Typically, the chief marketing officer is the link among all the disciplines; he or she hires specialists from each field and weaves them together, ensuring they are acting to achieve the company's larger objectives of sales, brand reputation, hiring, employee retention, and more.

Job security is in short supply for chief marketing officers because companies aren't measuring the right results—they're seeing the department as an expense instead of an investment.

The chief marketing officer typically stays on the job for 42 months, and that's a long time. In 2010, that was the longest tenure recorded in six years, when Spencer Stuart[1] began monitoring for this role.

The chief marketing officer hires Web, public relations, corporate communication, search, and advertising professionals, but rarely do they interact with one other. They each are comfortable in silos, doing what they know best. Because of the lack of integration across disciplines, the advertising professional might think public relations only does media relations. The public relations professional might think search is all black hat. And search might think direct mail is old, stodgy, and ineffective. The disciplines don't know what the others are doing, which won't work in the marketing round.

The birth of the marketing round at your company might mean the death of the title of chief marketing officer. But the leader of the round still must be a true strategist with firsthand knowledge of as many communication disciplines as possible.

The Forms of Media

The traditional forms of media for marketing and communication include public relations, advertising, direct mail, email, and some sort of Web strategy—even if it's just a Web site. In today's world you have to add inbound marketing, blogging, content marketing, search engine optimization, social media, search engine marketing, and more.

Each of those platforms exists for a different reason. Yet companies make the same mistake over and over: They use the same message across all platforms.

Each type of media serves a different purpose; the messages they carry should be completely different.

Say you want a series of webinars to generate leads for the sales team. There's one campaign, working toward one goal, but you have a wide array of tools and messages at your disposal:

1. The advertising department buys some Facebook or banner ads.

2. Your direct professional sends a postcard to your database, announcing the series with a save-the-date.

3. The public relations team creates a news release and does some publicity with event listings and trade publications.

4. The social media expert uses Twitter, Facebook, LinkedIn, Google+, and more to engage the community in not only gaining attendance but perhaps even crowdsourcing ideas or speakers.

5. The email professional executes a campaign that drips a prepro-duced set of messages to its audiences.

6. Perhaps you even announce on your blog or through other content.

Combining approaches increases your chance of effectiveness, and it also recognizes that people absorb information in many ways.

Let's review each of the tools within paid, earned, and owned media.

Paid Media

Paid media, according to ClickZ, is "exactly as it sounds. Marketers buy media, usually in the form of impressions, to affect sales. Some call this 'marketer-generated media,' but the old description works just fine. In the context of video, paid media may come in the form of the pre-roll, post-roll, or official sponsor link."[2]

The adage is that 50 percent of your media spend is wasted—you just don't know which half.[3] But paid media still plays an important role in building a brand, creating credibility, and driving sales.

Earned Media

Earned media typically means media relations.

Public relations professionals used to spend years developing relationships with reporters, journalists, editors, and producers, working to facilitate sto-ries that helped their companies or clients.

But with the technology age, traditional media outlets closed and many of the people whom public relations experts spent their entire careers building relationships with were out of jobs.

Though traditional media relations must continue with those who remain, its definition must expand to include building relationships with bloggers and social media influencers.

Owned Media

Owned media, according to Forrester, is "a channel you control. There is fully owned media (like your Web site or blog) and partially owned media (like a Facebook fan page or Twitter account). Owned media creates brand portability. Now you can extend your brand's presence beyond your Web site so it exists in many places across the Web—specifically through social media sites and unique communities. In a recession in which marketing budgets are being cut by 20 percent, the ability to communicate directly with consumers who *want* to engage with your brand through long-term relationships can be invaluable."[4]

Whether your owned media is blogging, white papers, eBooks, webinars, podcasts, video campaigns, or email marketing, it should reside on something you own, such as your Web site or blog. Then you lend that content and community to outlying networks such as Twitter, Facebook, and Google+.

Examples of the Forms of Media

To make forms of media work together, you must understand how they support each other.

Paid media helps jump-start owned media. The owned media grows and sustains earned media. The growth of earned media reduces the need for paid media, driving costs down.

In Table 2.1, paid, earned, and owned media is defined to help you understand each and to jumpstart your knowledge to become a true strategist.

Table 2.1   Forms of Media

Paid	Earned	Owned
Television	Media Relations	Print Materials
Radio	Word of Mouth	Social Media
Print	Trade Organizations	Blog
Web	Organic Search	Content (white papers, eBooks, etc.)

Paid	Earned	Owned
Social Media		Posters and Flyers
Direct Mail		Web
Outdoor (billboards, transit ads, etc.)		Email
Point-of-Purchase		Mobile
Paid Search		Videos
Sponsorships		Podcasts
Affiliate Marketing		Webinars
		Infographics
		Gamification

Pros and Cons of Each Medium

Each medium has its own set of pros and cons. Understanding them is key to using each effectively.

Paid Media

Paid media, while traditionally thought of as TV, radio, and print advertising, has grown to include many more avenues for getting a message across.

Following are the pros and cons of each paid media tactic.

Television

Pros:

- Reaches masses of people at once
- As a visual, provides better retention
- Quick and short bits of information
- Allows for measurement through specific URLs and toll-free numbers

Cons:

- Expensive to produce
- Expensive to buy time
- People don't like ads
- DVR existence

Radio

Pros:

- Easy to target specific audiences
- Less expensive than other paid media

Cons:

- People switch stations during commercial breaks
- Often playing while people are participating in other activities

Print

Pros:

- More detailed information than TV or radio
- Tailored messages for specific audiences
- Not as expensive as other forms of paid media

Cons:

- Readership is dwindling for print publications
- People flip through ads

Web

Pros:

- Web is the first place people go for information
- Search engine marketing, or pay-per-click, is effective
- Customizable information based on target audiences

- Easy to share
- Can use in other forms of paid media

Cons:

- Requires Internet access
- Audience is required to use the Web

Social Media

Pros:

- Inexpensive form of sponsoring messages on the social platforms
- Messages shared by trusted friends are more accepted
- Allows people to engage with your company
- Information easily spread
- Instant and real-time
- Can target people very easily

Cons:

- People don't like their streams full of ads
- Ads violate the integrity of the social platforms
- You can't force a message to spread
- Less control over the message if it does spread
- Information overload

Direct Mail

Pros:

- Can buy mailing lists that are very specific to the types of people you're targeting
- Allows a personalized message
- Provides an outlet for promotional items

Cons:

- People rarely open "junk" mail
- Has to be highly creative to be opened
- Expensive
- Not "green" in today's digital age

Outdoor

Pros:

- Provides a cool way to use new tools, such as QR codes
- Easy way to reach commuters
- Has a built-in audience

Cons:

- Expensive
- Cannot provide a lot of information
- Message must be understood within seconds

Point-of-Purchase

Pros:

- Catches people when they are thinking about your product
- Allows testing of different messages with target audience
- Has the perception of being endorsed by the store
- Can provide discounts or other offers

Cons:

- Must regularly change messages and offers
- Must have someone on hand several times a week to stock product
- Stores may not always want to participate

Paid Search

Pros:

- Faster than organic search
- Allows for experimentation
- Creation of unique landing pages allows a call-to-action and tracking
- Easy-to-measure conversion rates
- Can set own budget

Cons:

- Less than one-fourth of people use paid search results in their first try at accessing information
- Can be expensive if you don't know what you're doing
- May not get as many clicks as with organic search

Sponsorships

Pros:

- Allows people to build a connection with your company or brand
- Builds a positive image
- Has the perception of being endorsed by organization
- Builds brand awareness
- Builds goodwill
- Provides exclusivity
- Generates positive publicity

Cons:

- Obligations can deter from learning opportunities (at conferences or trade shows)
- Can create a lot of extra work
- Ties you to a controversy if it develops with the organization (or celebrity)

- Lack of industry-wide standardization
- Time and labor intensive

Affiliate Marketing

Pros:

- Easy to set up and get started
- Low start-up costs
- Provides an additional revenue stream
- A wider place to sell your products or services

Cons:

- Low level of control
- High competition
- Target audience not locked in
- Can be expensive if you don't know what you're doing
- High level of unethical behavior among merchants

Earned Media

Earned media is traditionally thought of as public relations and/or publicity. It now has grown to include influencers, bloggers, and customers.

Following are the pros and cons of each earned media tactic.

Media Relations

Pros:

- Third-party credibility reigns supreme
- People still read articles, listen to radio programs, and watch television news
- Not perceived as an ad
- Don't have to pay for space

Cons:

- Relationships with journalists waning
- Every week, in the United States alone, two media outlets go out of business
- Hard to measure, other than providing a good ego boost
- Time for a professional's help is expensive

Word of Mouth

Pros:

- Free
- Builds trust
- Can guide messages to enhance exposure
- Develops brand ambassadors

Cons:

- Potential for negative comments
- Can't be controlled
- Hard to create
- Not efficient for big audiences

Trade Organizations

Pros:

- Can do live or virtual
- Allows you to meet with several prospects and customers at one time
- Provides an opportunity to meet with media
- Creates the face-to-face opportunity missing through many digital avenues

Cons:

- Expensive
- Attendance waning

- People don't want to be sold
- Return on investment lower than with other marketing tools

Organic Search

Pros:

- Longer lasting than paid search
- Clicked on more than paid search
- Converts at least as well as paid search
- Has more latency
- No cost
- More text space available

Cons:

- Takes a long time to rank
- Content is the single best way to create organic search, but you need lots of it

Owned Media

Owned media is the new sibling to paid and earned media. No longer do you have to rely solely on big media buys or third-party influencers to tell your story; you can do it in a creative way that is valuable to your target audiences.

Following are the pros and cons of each owned media tactic.

Collateral Materials

Pros:

- Conveys information about complex topics
- Useful as follow-up to meetings
- Doesn't compete with ads
- Useful for frequently asked questions

Cons:

- Expensive
- Not a "green" option
- Most people use the Web rather than a brochure for information

Social Media

Pros:

- Builds online relationships with customers and prospects
- Helps discover brand ambassadors and loyalists
- Builds brand loyalty
- Provides a way to get feedback about your products and services
- The tools are free
- Easy to track your competitors
- More effectively serve your current customers
- Easy to network 24/7, from anywhere, and with large audiences
- More exposure to your company
- Provides global access
- Fosters community

Cons:

- Time intensive
- Building relationships with humans takes time
- You lose control
- The return on investment is delayed
- Negative information spreads more quickly
- Does not conform to traditional marketing methods
- More exposure to your company
- It's distracting
- Everything online lives there forever
- Must be active daily

Blog

Pros:

- Single best way to generate, nurture, and convert leads
- Tools are free
- Fosters community
- Provides a creative way to promote your company
- Can blog from anywhere with an Internet connection
- Provides lots of organic search
- Develops credibility and thought leadership
- Can be created in written, audio, or video format

Cons:

- Time and labor intensive
- Consistency is key, so it must have new content frequently
- Blogger(s) must be passionate or it won't work
- Takes a while to gain a loyal readership and steady traffic

Content

Pros:

- Technical accuracy
- Provides opportunity for internal and external audiences to provide feedback
- Can be updated very quickly
- Provides lots of organic search
- Generates leads
- Easy to create
- No cost to reproduce (if doing it digitally)

Cons:

- Easy to get wrapped up in writing for the business and not the audience

- Must be written by someone who can write in an engaging and conversational way
- If using multiple writers, voice is difficult to maintain
- If not part of someone's job, it won't get done

Posters and Fliers

Pros:

- Generates awareness
- Inexpensive
- Can be put in places where target audiences already congregate
- If they're attractive, people will want to buy and use in homes or offices

Cons:

- High probability of being stolen or taken down
- Stores and other locations may not want to post
- May need to be reposted often
- May incur some design costs

Web Site

Pros:

- Provides an interactive way to engage with customers and prospects
- Easy to track and measure
- Allows you to maintain control of your messages
- Can incorporate social networks, video, and more

Cons:

- A necessity in doing business today
- Must be mobile-ready
- Understanding the pros and cons of Flash or HTML5 necessary

- Must stay on top of trends, such as HTML5, social media, and gamification (a game quality to your content, Web site, or blog that encourages people to return)

Email

Pros:

- Quick and easy delivery
- Can test different times of day and week to send
- Can test different messages
- Easy to track and measure
- Inexpensive
- Targeted

Cons:

- Must understand the CAN-SPAM Act
- Easily ignored
- Information overload
- Requires expertise in designing optimized email templates

Mobile

Pros:

- Instant results
- Easy to work with and to understand
- Convenient for your customers and prospects
- Allows personalized interaction
- Easy to track and measure
- Payments made easy
- Microblogging made easy

Cons:

- Still being explored so not lots of case studies from which to learn
- Lack of platform standardization
- Privacy issues
- Lack of navigation may create issues

Videos

Pros:

- Very searchable on search engines
- People are visual learners
- YouTube is the second-largest search engine
- Easy to embed in Web site and/or blog

Cons:

- Some initial costs (camera and editing software)
- Hard to create good content—talking heads don't work unless the person is extremely charismatic
- Need editing skills

Podcasts

Pros:

- Fairly easy to create
- Great for people who don't have time to read
- Can download to music player
- Listen on the go
- Some people learn by listening

Cons:

- Need some editing skills
- Doesn't allow for two-way conversation

- Not searchable in search engines
- More difficult to measure

Webinars

Pros:

- Provides a visual way for people to learn
- Visually and audibly engaging
- Can record so people can download if they can't make it to the live event
- Generates and nurtures leads
- Can convert leads
- Useful features, such as polls, live chat, desktop share, and even video options
- Speakers can be highly influential people within your industry

Cons:

- Software is expensive and difficult to use
- Must have a polished speaker
- Must create rehearsal time
- An agenda is a necessity
- Must leave room for Q&A, preferably throughout

Infographics

Pros:

- Visually appealing
- Currently popular
- Easy to share and distribute
- Able to show concepts and information in a fun and engaging way
- Search engine friendly

Cons:

- Becoming overused
- A designer is a necessity
- Without a great concept, it won't work
- Time intensive

Gamification

Pros:

- Tip of the iceberg for something larger in the digital ecosystem
- Makes buying more pleasurable

Cons:

- Really unsophisticated and oversimplified right now
- If done poorly initially, opportunity will be lost
- In its infancy

Taking It One Step at a Time

Looking at all the options you're responsible for sifting through, it's easy to get overwhelmed. Where do you start? How will you staff? Where do you get the resources?

The answer to all these questions is not all at once. People crawl before they walk. Then they run. And then they grow up, navigate high school, and further their education for their chosen path in life. It takes time.

The marketing round can be looked at the same way.

Crawl

More than likely you already have a digital monitoring and listening program in place. If you don't, buy a social media book (such as *Groundswell* or *Social Media ROI*) and set one up. You can't create the marketing-round plan or begin to execute without this very important competitive intelligence.

Crawling is the phase where you establish your infrastructure.

Who is in your marketing round—one person from each discipline? Or are you smaller, with just a few of you representing everything? Assign roles and then take an inventory of your resources. Decide what your first priority is, and then create a 90-day plan that allows you to crawl toward it.

For instance, Vistaprint, a global online printing company, knew that one of its key challenges was to provide small-batch print orders to small and emerging businesses.

Vistaprint's marketing round decided to create a multipronged advertising campaign to speak specifically to that target audience. Working with its advertising and digital teams, it developed an online ad campaign of email, text, and banner ads on third-party Web sites, plus some pay-per-click ads.

Then the digital team added an idea that it hoped would make the campaign go viral: It offered 250 free business cards to anyone, regardless of whether he or she made another purchase.

Two billion of those business cards are being passed around in the United States, each carrying the Vistaprint logo and tag line. That one Vistaprint campaign created the opportunity for 66 percent growth in new customers—all of whom started out with free business cards.

That was some pretty spectacular crawling.

Walk

Now it's time for the next steps. You've tested a few things, you've created benchmarks, you have some confidence about what works and what doesn't. Now leverage that knowledge: Use technology to your benefit, produce content, participate in conversations, use multiple platforms for communication, and measure results to the marketing round.

A famous case study for the walking phase of the marketing round is Will It Blend from Blendtec.

First the crawl: The CMO wanted to get the word out to consumers (as opposed to restaurateurs) about how great the Blendtec blenders are. He made YouTube videos in his garage of Blendtec blenders blending up anything and everything—an iPhone, a skeleton, glow sticks.

The walking phase: He created multiple platforms, used technology to his advantage, and participated in the resulting conversation. People followed the videos on the corporate Web site, on YouTube, and on Facebook. Nearly 100,000 Facebook fans participated by suggesting what should get whirled up in the next video.

The CMO had less than a shoestring budget, but he wanted to get the word out about how great the Blendtec blenders are, especially among consumers because their core restaurant audience was already covered.

One weekend, at home in his garage, he wondered what kinds of things the blenders would blend and began experimenting. He's tried everything from an iPhone and an iPad to a skeleton and glow sticks.

He records video of the things Blendtec will blend, uploads them to YouTube, and also posts them to the corporate Web site.

Without the advantage of a marketing round, he crawled. Then he walked by using technology to his advantage and used multiple platforms to advance the messaging. From there he began to participate in conversations and opened the discussion to his network, who opened it to their network, and so on.

Although you may not have something that goes viral like Will It Blend, you can use your walking phase to test ideas, use different technologies, and deploy various platforms to see what sticks with your audiences.

Run

Your marketing round is working efficiently. You're measuring results. You're refining and improving. Now it's time to begin engaging, responding multiple times every day, and leveraging employees outside of the marketing round.

During your marketing-round meeting, ask the following questions:

- How can HR use the social networks to recruit candidates?
- How can customer service use a chat feature on the Web site, the social networks, the telephone, and email to provide immediate response?
- How can sales network with customers and prospects before they attend a trade show or travel to a new city?
- How can R&D use focus groups, crowdsourcing, and market research to innovate and develop new products?

- How can legal keep the policies and employee code of conduct current?
- How can the executive team get in front of customers on a daily or weekly basis by using technology?
- How can you reach beyond the marketing round to produce content and develop your owned media program?
- How can customers help create content?
- How can the marketing-round support all of these needs in the most efficient way?

There are plenty of examples of how companies are leveraging employees, beyond the marketing round: Five Guys' employee incentive program drives customer satisfaction and word of mouth marketing. IBM has hundreds of employees blogging. Starbuck employees give free drinks to customers at stores using coupons. Habitat for Humanity workers use their intranet to connect multiple times each day. Geek Squad employees at Best Buy drive automobiles that have signage painted on the car touting its tech services. Zappos has 500 employees on Twitter.

You may not be as large as these organizations, but there are ideas, tips, and techniques you can shamelessly steal from such companies that leverage their employees in the marketing round.

Fly

And now you're at the point that you can fly. You will scale and integrate the marketing round into all business functions. Everything you do is measurable and tracked to gross margins. By the time you get here, the marketing round will be seen as an investment rather than an expense.

Exercises

To determine which assets you have, which need to be added, and which can wait until later (or never), work with the marketing round on Table 2.2.

Table 2.2   Marketing Round Assets

Media	Going to Use?	Crawl, Walk, Run, or Fly Phase	Responsible
EXAMPLE: Inbound Marketing	Yes	Walk	Marketing, PR, sales
Television			
Radio			
Print			
Web			
Social Media			
Direct Mail			
Outdoor			
Point-of-Purchase			
Paid Search			
Sponsorships			
Affiliate Marketing			
Media Relations			
Word of Mouth			
Trade Organizations			
Organic Search			
Print Materials			
Social Media			
Blog			
Content			
Posters and Fliers			
Web site			
Email			
Mobile			

Table 2.2 Marketing Round Assets

Media	Going to Use?	Crawl, Walk, Run, or Fly Phase	Responsible
Videos			
Podcasts			
Webinars			
Infographics			
Gamification			

Endnotes

1. www.spencerstuart.com/about/media/65/.

2. www.clickz.com/clickz/column/1718641/the-official-cgm-glossary.

3. *"Half the money I spend on advertising is wasted; the trouble is I don't know which half." —John Wanamaker, U.S. department store merchant (1838–1922)*

4. http://blogs.forrester.com/interactive_marketing/2009/12/defining-earned-owned-and-paid-media.html.

3

Understand Stakeholders and the Competitive Landscape

An uninformed company only thinks it knows what its stakeholders want. It goes about blindly dictating to its market without testing for demand or price tolerance. And it expects sales to magically occur.

It may as well throw services against a wall, like mud, and see what sticks.

Research and preparation are the most important first steps for a communicator who wants the marketing round to find the right communication path. When the round understands the market dynamics in play, it (as a group) is better able to make decisions about strategy and tactics.

The two major categories of research are quantitative and qualitative. Quantitative methods focus on numerical and statistical data—percentages, numbers, and demographics are hallmarks of quantitative research. Qualitative research uses interviews, tonality, content themes, and other forms of subjective data to understand customers' psychological decision-making processes.

A marketing round has many resources for market research, whether it is purchased from firms such as Forrester and Gartner, gathered from customers in focus groups, or collected through their use of social media. Research falls into several categories:

- **Competitive:** An examination of market leaders' positioning, offerings, and marketing approaches.

- **Stakeholder:** Understanding the wants and needs of a customer group, their media use patterns, and their reaction to previous offerings.

- **Historical:** An analysis of how an industry has performed with traditional players, with new entrants, under economic strain, and with new technologies.

- **Inward-focused:** An examination of stakeholder behavior on a company's Web site and brutal assessments of its strengths and weaknesses.

Consider how Kellogg's used market research to expand its United Kingdom–based Crunchy Nut brand in 2003. Cereal makers are in a constant fight to expand market share in a limited, established growth marketplace. Kellogg's existing Crunchy Nut Cornflakes franchise was a $103 million business at that time. In 2003, Kellogg's launched a brand extension: Crunchy Nut Clusters in two flavors, Milk Chocolate Curls and Honey and Nut, creating another $33 million in annual sales. Given that success, the company decided to explore a new brand extension in the mid-2000s using market research to inform its efforts.

Kellogg's began its new Crunchy Nut effort with research available through books, journals, the Internet, and government statistics. The company researched industry innovation and gathered information about the newest flavors and food trends in various countries. From there, they used focus groups to explore cereal possibilities that fit the flavors and trends yet stayed within their brand. This armed Kellogg's with several workable paths for new cereals.

Kellogg's took the focus groups' favorites and created new packaging for several of the products. They surveyed cereal buyers to determine which flavors and brands would be best received, and they settled on Crunchy Nut Bites. The company manufactured the product and ran a test phase before full market launch. The test validated the new brand, and in its first full year of production Crunchy Nut Bites generated $11 million in sales.[1]

Kellogg's made a major investment in the development and launch of Crunchy Nut Bites. But don't be discouraged if your marketing round doesn't have access to a massive market research budget. Not all forms of research cost thousands of dollars, and even the leanest organizations can use freely available survey and search technologies to question their customers about needs and perceptions, to find relevant conversations on the Internet, and to analyze their competitors' offerings.

Commonly called a Strengths, Weaknesses, Opportunities, and Threats (SWOT) analysis, this basic form of research can serve as the starting point for a meaningful conversation among your marketing round as it begins to plan a campaign. Before delving into building your SWOT report, let's discuss uses of market research in forging marketing strategy, some recommendations to begin research, and competitive analysis.

Branding and Its Role in the Marketing Round

Branding a product or a company is the process of making a promise of value and crafting messages designed to resonate with customers. It is the company's commitment to stakeholders. That brand commitment is communicated visually and verbally by the marketing round and its immediate and extended team of marketing professionals, and it is borne out, hopefully, by actual customer experience. Brands that stand the test of time are those that deliver on their commitment and back up the message with actual marketplace reputation among customers.

But if the product or service falls short of the company's marketing promise, it creates a gap between the company and the customer. That gap breeds bad word of mouth, slows sales, and can result in the complete collapse of the marketing initiative.

That's why testing your offering with active market research is essential. Ask potential clients whether product performance is living up to its promise. If it isn't, fix it. Fix it either by changing the product or by changing the promise.

In many cases marketers are handed an established brand, and they don't have the luxury to engage in an "extreme makeover." Nor should they, in most cases.

Ford Motor Company would be foolish to rebrand its Mustang line. Would the storied muscle car that was born in 1964 work if they called it the Cheetah? No. Would a "softer" horse icon for its logo go over well? No again. The Mustang stands the test of time. Ford should not (and will not) rebrand the Mustang anytime soon.

Branding has a vital role in any marketing effort, and diligent research helps brand strategists forge the essence of an offering as they seek to place it in an irresistible position in the marketplace.

But comprehensive strategies go much, much further. They get into the weeds of budgeting and resource allocation; planning media buys; timing news releases; building measurement programs to monitor performance, adapt campaigns, and report results; creating editorial calendars for content development; strategically timing direct mail drops or email marketing campaigns; and on and on. The actual business of a marketing strategy is much more comprehensive than the creative excitement of branding.

Listening and Research First

Many organizations don't listen to their stakeholders; they think they already understand their needs and wants. Their marketing organizations start talking at customers—diffusing messages, statements, and random facts. Or, worst of all, showering online communities with links to its news releases.

Talking at customers and stakeholders without listening to them is the equivalent of marching into a networking event with a fistful of business cards, and mercilessly delivering elevator pitches. What a turnoff. If you don't engage in actual conversations, you're likely to short-circuit lead-generation opportunities and make a very negative first impression.

Many organizations are not used to listening. Historically, they've done most of the talking, and use of traditional media does not lend itself to listening. With each year of social media maturation, however, brands have suffered significant reputation damage for failing to listen to their markets.

Strong networkers listen. They learn about their conversation partners. They learn how they can help them; they build rapport. Through those conversations, they learn how their product or service is most useful. They then follow through, tailoring their efforts accordingly.

Social media, as a method of listening, is one of the great capabilities added to the marketing round since the initial dot-com era. Using social media to actively learn from existing communities, or to passively mine data and information for insights, is something even the most conservative of brands engage in. Others go further, turning it into an active customer interaction channel.

Take Virgin America. The airline uses Twitter to keep tabs on how its services are working for its customers—a typical use of social media. But Virgin America has taken it a step further, using social media to interact with customers online and communicate with them when cancellations or other issues arise. Virgin America answers in-flight tweets sent over its in-air Gogo Wi-Fi service, and it rebooks customers who have missed their flights through multiple interactive channels.

The result of using social media to listen and respond? The net promoter score of Virgin American rivals that of Apple. Word of mouth, such as Twitter, Facebook, and other channels, is so strong for its brand that Virgin America has decided to forgo television advertising. Its markets are already served—by its customers—through its social media efforts.

Social media isn't the only place to listen:

- Customer-provided input is a key source of information.
- News roundups and trade publications offer general marketplace discussions and insights into competitors and technological developments.
- Trade shows and conferences are fantastic places to take the pulse of an industry.
- Companies' stock performance can tell you who the public winners are in a competitive field.

As data unfolds, listening becomes a form of market research. The two become interchangeable—listening inspires questions and the need to find out more about certain aspects of the data set.

Usually, listening information gets parsed into types of data sets. One set is customer- and stakeholder-related: Who are they and what are their demographics—age, gender, income, living situations? Which offerings do they prefer and why? What's driving their product choices? What are the gaps they want companies to fill?

Another set involves the competition: Which brands are winning customers' hearts and minds? Why have they succeeded? What are the opportunities for your marketing round to stand out?

Truly listening to the reactions to an offering and to perceptions of a brand can be tough. Companies, and their marketing teams, are made up of people, and people can be easily upset by one negative comment out of 100. Your marketing round has to steel itself for this moment.

A courageous and intelligent organization will listen to what is being said, or not said, by its customers. It will be calm in its willingness to hear about its efforts to date, and take the feedback to heart. Dismissing and denying the public's perceptions and comments leaves reams of valuable data out of the decision-making process. And without accurate data, a marketing round cannot make decisions and choices with precision and confidence.

Listening provides some initial data points for what will be your SWOT analysis. Some marketers start the report at this stage, classifying the data loosely into strength, weakness, opportunity, and threat categories. They may even brief the marketing round to see whether the data gathered so far has brought up new questions or market insights.

Listening also tells you what you don't know—gaps and unanswered questions toward which you can direct your research. Uncovering the data points necessary to resolve such issues provides clarity for your SWOT analysis, and that will inform your marketing round's discussion.

Competitive Analysis

Some believe they should focus on their own core actions and grow a bigger pie for the whole industry, and others see competitors as all-out enemies. Whichever side you're on, it's helpful to have context when evaluating your competitors' successes and failures in the marketplace.

There are some marketing actions all companies have to take to become viable. These include publishing a Web site; creating news stories; initiating social media efforts; developing advertisements for print, broadcast, interactive, and/or search; and creating content and publicly available newsletters.

Analyze your competitors' marketing—see which efforts work well, and understand why stakeholders like them: What is their primary messaging? Why does or doesn't it work? Which products or services compete directly against your own? What are the price points? Are there public partnerships that help distribute their offerings? How loyal are their customers?

If you are competing against U.S. publicly traded companies, look at their 10-K and 10-Q SEC filings. Such companies are required by law to inform investors about prospects and threats—a great way to get intelligence about your competitors' actions and about general market risks.

Record this analysis in an easy-to-access document, perhaps a spread-sheet on a shared workspace if you're dealing with more than a handful of competitors. Organize your competition by threat level—some are more successful than others, some will be head-to-head rivals in sales situations. Ranking the players in the total marketplace will allow your marketing round to focus energy on combating the players that pose the biggest threats to your sales and viability.

Competitive focus allows your marketing round to see what kinds of offerings and products will meet consumer demand, what it can do to be different, and how it can capitalize on weaknesses or gaps. Your effort should be different from the competition and adaptable in form and price by customers who will clearly use it. Good marketing puts a product or service into the market that's almost undefeatable.

Strengths, Weaknesses, Opportunities, and Threats Report

Your company has an objective—it might be a specific initiative, or it might be general market performance for the year. That objective is the focus of your SWOT analysis. State it clearly and keep it in mind above all else when writing your SWOT report.

Divide your data into the four categories of strengths and weaknesses, which are internal variables, and opportunities and threats, which examine external market factors:

- Strengths: What internal assets or behaviors give your business an advantage in the marketplace?
- Weaknesses: Which internal defects and issues can prevent you from succeeding?
- Opportunities: Are there external factors you can take advantage of?
- Threats: Who and what can stop your business from succeeding?

SWOT analysis became popular in the 1970s through Albert Humphrey's work at Stanford University examining Fortune 500 data. SWOT is sometimes criticized for causing companies to focus too much on some aspects of the research, but it is still a common baseline for project- and corporate-based market research.

A SWOT analysis can be presented as a written report, as spreadsheets, or as simple charts, depending on the size of the project, the size of the competitive field, and the size of your budget. Whatever the size or depth of a SWOT analysis, it is always helpful to have a summary chart. A bulleted chart can serve as an executive summary or as the complete SWOT analysis in situations that demand brevity. Your colleagues in the marketing round also will appreciate it—not everyone has time to read dozens of pages of market data and analysis.

Table 3.1 is a sample SWOT analysis chart that illustrates how to begin organizing your research into the four categories.

Table 3.1 Sample SWOT Analysis

Strengths	Weaknesses
• Online delivery • Early adopters' positive talk • Low cost • Customer referrals largest source of leads • Customers voluntarily talk about product online	• Acme has 100x the revenue in its store • No publicly identified thought leader • Media is not actively covering market shift
Opportunities	**Threats**
• Use electronic distribution to undercut the market • No competitor is effectively blogging • Rewards programs encourage further customer-driven word of mouth	• Low marketing budget; can't afford advertising • Other venture-capital-based start-ups (Alpha and Beta) • Acme buys a competitor • Acme invests in new market

Testing the Waters

Despite all the research and all the marketing history available, there are too many intangibles, too many variables to ever know how a market will truly react to an idea. Sometimes you just have to dip your toe in the waters with an initial foray—focus groups, invite-only "alpha groups," or an announcement of intent.

A classic example of this was Southwest Airlines' decision to blog in 2007 about a potential seating-policy change. The revised seating would have created a business-class assigned section. Would have. Online customers, more than 700 on that blog post alone, responded with disdain. They did not want to lose their ability to choose their own seat based on check-in order.

Hot water for Southwest, indeed. But rather than simply caving to the social media clamor, Southwest acknowledged its new seating policy was not ready for market. They published an apology and committed to taking customers' views into consideration. In essence, Southwest listened and responded, instead of having an unfortunate or short-sighted reaction to a public corporate crisis.

The airline then created its A, B, and C priority seating system—a workable compromise that met revenue needs, addressed business customers' wants, and appeased the loyal customer base.

Testing the waters for a specific effort can save a company from public embarrassment. Focus groups, blind surveys, and panels of willing participants—online and offline—can not only foreshadow a product's eventual success, but also offer insights into positioning and marketing tactics that can break open a campaign.

Continuing that well-built measurement program throughout an effort gives you a perpetual source of data about your customers and the marketplace. (Chapter 11, "Measure Results to Dollars and Cents," deals specifically with using measurement as a diagnostic tool to continue evolving your marketing campaign.)

Communities and markets do not always react as you have anticipated—negative situations will arise. In those situations, forewarned is forearmed. Being in touch with your customers and stakeholders, listening to them, and considering different scenarios makes their pulse easier to read. That makes it easier for your marketing-round table to understand and evolve as necessary.

Exercises

To develop your SWOT, you need to do some reconnaissance with the marketplace and your competitors.

First work with the marketing round to complete Table 3.2. List your top three to five competitors, the products or services they offer, the marketing-round assets they have (see Table 3.2), and which phase you think they're working in. If they don't seem to have a marketing round or haven't entered a phase, just enter N/A.

Table 3.2   Competitive Analysis

Competitor	Product/Service	Asset(s)	Crawl, Walk, Run, Fly Phase

Now you can complete your SWOT analysis by filling in Table 3.3.

Table 3.3   Develop Your SWOT Analysis

Strengths	Weaknesses
Opportunities	Threats

Endnotes

1. The Times 100, "Kellogg's: New Products from Market
    Research," *Times Newspaper Limited*, 2010, 53–56.

4

Marketing: Tools, Tactics, Sequencing, and Timing

When carpenters build an addition to a house, they create a plan, get the materials, and gather their tools—from saws and sandpaper to hammers and screwdrivers. The carpenters carefully sequence their activities: foundation, framing, drywall, and finishing. Proper order ensures the addition is a good fit with the original structure and will stand the test of time.

Like the carpenters, the marketing round has to understand how each tool affects a stakeholder and where it fits with other tools in the larger marketing mix. Yet when most marketers start thinking strategy, the first thing they do is reach for their favorite tools—regardless of whether they are the best tools for the job. They're familiar with, say, direct marketing techniques, or with putting on an event. But a marketing campaign rarely ends with a news conference, nor does it begin with a customized thank-you letter. Choose your tools for their fit with your strategic objective, not for your comfort level.

Another classic mistake is to select tools because they are new or talked about frequently in the media. This "shiny object syndrome" is a fascination with the newest, hippest tool rather than a strategic selection of media and methods to achieve an objective.

In 2011, social media such as Google+ and Instagram fit this description. They're all the rage, and many marketers are blindly saying, "We need a Google+ strategy." They may, indeed, be the right tools for your marketing effort. But without understanding how they will help you reach your objective (if at all), it's foolhardy—and a waste of resources—to dive in.

The marketing round should select the company's marketing approach based on four factors:

1. Key performance indicators.

2. The corresponding marketing objectives, whether they be lead generation, branding, or both.

3. Stakeholders and how you can communicate with them.

4. Capacity to market to them, specifically your budget and your human resources.

These components form the foundation of the marketing round's strategy and dictate your possible approaches and the tools you can use.

The Four Approaches to Choosing Tactics

Marketing strategy can be compared to military strategy. Many marketers use military terminology to discuss their campaigns. Words such as target, campaigns, supply chain, and strategies are rooted in army nomenclature. This is not a coincidence.

Unlike a military strategist, you don't want to attack people or treat your stakeholders like enemies. But you do want to realize objectives in your campaign. You do want people to buy your product or service, and to advocate for your brand. That allows a company to win a market and defeat its competitors. In that sense, there is much to learn from military strategists.

One of the greatest texts on military strategy is *The Book of Five Rings,* by seventeenth-century Japanese samurai Miyamoto Musashi. The wisdom collected from his decades of victory is packed into *Five Rings,* and several of his battle tenets are relevant to the marketing executive's fight to communicate a company's message and achieve victory.

In the "Water Book," or the second ring, Musashi discusses five primary approaches to strategic engagement: the middle (or direct), above, below (the groundswell), and the left and right sides (combined to one: flanking). Independently or sequenced, the primary approaches form a baseline to approaching marketing strategies.

Figure 4.1 shows you how "Water Book" describes the second ring, which can be applied to the marketing round's strategic engagement.

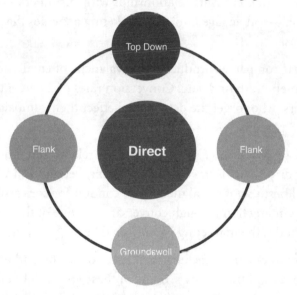

Figure 4.1 *The four approaches applied to marketing.*

The rest of this chapter delves into understanding the necessary preparation for selecting your approach or combination of approaches. This directly applies the knowledge you have gained about your stakeholders through market research.

Direct Community Interaction with Stakeholders

"The Middle attitude is the heart of attitudes," Musashi wrote. "If we look at strategy on a broad scale, the Middle attitude is the seat of the commander, with the other...attitudes following the commander."

Whenever possible, marketers and communicators should directly inter-act with their primary stakeholders. Whether the topic is sales, donations, input on ideas, agreement on civil actions, public resolution of customer issues, customer reviews, or other actions, direct communication is most likely to produce outcomes, and quickly. There is no interference between organization and customer. There is no media. There are no bloggers to speculate. There is no issue or regulation to circumnavigate. Done well, it's one-to-one marketing at its best.

Direct approaches, more often than not, require relationships. Rare is the person who will openly accept a marketing solicitation out of the blue. Instead, companies cultivate relationships with customers—current, past, and potential—and engage in direct marketing activities that strengthen relationships.

Usually what companies produce is an avalanche of emails and junk mail that consumers trash or delete. Conversion rates of 2 percent are cherished by marketers, who forget the detrimental effect their campaign has had on the other 98 percent.

Social media, however, is a powerful tool for relationship building and for interacting directly with stakeholders. The marketing round should make highest and best use of social media as a conduit for conversation—direct community interaction through conversation is one of the most powerful middle attitudes the marketing round can take.

Other direct interactions include shelf space or stores, and live events such as conferences and trade shows. Some of these approaches are more effec-tive than others, depending on their execution. And realistically, integrating several approaches may be necessary for success.

Lands' End is a textbook example of the direct marketing success on sev-eral levels. It started in 1963 selling casual goods to users through catalog marketing. The company adapted an attitude of being a "direct merchant" in 1978 with a primary focus on casual clothing. As the '80s dawned and waned, it grew to a $400-million-a-year company. It deployed an occasional advertising campaign, but the company's primary focus was direct market-ing, specifically catalog sales. In fact, when the company overordered mer-chandise in the late '80s, it marketed its way out of excess by printing an additional $2 million worth of catalogs.

In the '90s, Lands' End expanded into more diverse offerings, including converting their outlet stores to inlet stores, and then went into online direct marketing with the dot-com era. It rolled out unique offerings: oxford shirts designed by customers and 3D models of clothing. LandsEnd. com was a direct marketing hit, forging a second major channel for the company, with $200 million in sales by 2001. In addition, Lands' End operated select stores, called Lands' End Inlet. Sears bought Lands' End in 2002 for $2 billion in cash.

Top-Down Influence Approaches

"In the second approach with the long sword, from the Upper attitude cut the enemy just as he attacks," Musashi said. "In this method there are various changes in timing and spirit."

The top-down attitude is one in which media—events, PR, some types of advertising campaigns, and well-known influencers—are used to "inform" the marketplace about new products. The message comes to the marketplace from a position of authority, and the source hopes that the position of media voices, celebrities, and bloggers is enough to trickle down to the community and persuade it.

To command top-down attention, a company usually needs to have market leadership, whether as a thought leader or in market share. A successful public relations effort can launch a company into the leadership position, but there are dangers to such an effort—touting a product or service as top-of-the-line when it isn't can be disastrous.

A top-down campaign often is deployed to reach stakeholders that direct marketing cannot, or is launched to complement a direct marketing effort. It is a definitive statement, seeking to dominate a market from the outset; but its level of success depends on the marketplace's level of trust in the company, the product's capability to fulfill its marketing claims, and the community's readiness to accept the offering.

If the product or service launch is too early or too late for its market, it will be hard for a company to assume a leadership spot and drive interest. Similarly, if the product is pitched beyond its capability to deliver on the brand promise, the pitch will fail.

When the marketplace trusts an organization, it is more likely to accept a top-down approach. Apple masters this approach better than anyone. Every product announcement is like watching a symphony: What will Apple come up with next?

The announcements are a well-oiled marketing machine—the use of blogs to leak information, the use of media to report on blogs. The entire market watches which components the company is buying to guess which product will be launched next.

Until Steve Jobs passed away, the marketplace was always poised for the maverick tech titan to lead Apple's own onstage unveiling events, packed with journalists, bloggers, and industry insiders. Apple avoids major industry announcement fests, such as the annual Consumer Electronics Show, preferring to orchestrate its own events when it's convenient for the company, not the industry.

The launches at Apple are accompanied by traditional outdoor, print, and broadcast advertising buys; by in-store displays; and of course by signature packaging. Its Web site is tuned to announcements; launch day brings new, in-depth Web pages and videos explaining new products. It emails customers on launch day, encouraging them to buy. These advertisements and direct marketing campaigns, orchestrated with the public relations efforts, create a seamless multichannel, multitouch approach—one of the best integrated and repeatable marketing formulas the world has ever seen.

But the real reason Apple is able to achieve marketing nirvana with every launch is its products and services. The company launches products and services that are legendary for their research and design, and they are welcomed—and trusted—by technology lovers and consumers alike.

Likewise, Under Armour built its company with top-down approaches. The fledgling sportswear start-up was launched in 1996 with just $17,000 in sales, strictly by word of mouth (the groundswell approach). In 1997 that rose to $100,000. Then the company got its first big break. Oakland Raider quarterback Jeff George was photographed for the cover of USA Today in an Under Armour turtleneck. That picture triggered two major sales from Atlantic Coast Conference schools Georgia Tech and North Carolina.

Sales continued increasing as a result of fans and athletes watching the growing Under Armour brand break into the sports ranks. These sporting figures served as influencers, demonstrating the value of the brand.

But nothing drove sales quite like actor Jamie Foxx's appearance in *Any Given Sunday* in an Under Armour jockstrap. It fueled enough money for founder Kevin Plank to buy an ad in *ESPN Magazine*, which triggered $750,000 in sales. Today, Under Armour is a major sporting goods brand with close to $1 billion in sales.

A top-down approach should be an organization's primary tactic only when it can dominate a market, or when it cannot engage directly with a large community. Otherwise, it is better employed as a carefully targeted support tactic within a larger strategy.

The Groundswell

"In the third approach, adopt the Lower attitude, anticipating scooping up," Musashi said.

Not every company has the luxury of an established customer base for its products and services. Nor do all organizations have the resources to support advertising and promotional campaigns that blanket their marketplace.

One powerful and cost-effective, if difficult, method of spreading the word about a product or service is word of mouth—marketing to loyal customers by the individual, who shares with dozens, who keep the groundswell going until it is a major success.

The marketing round can help foster word of mouth by seeding conversations, fostering forward motion and upward sales—earning trust for its product by encouraging customers, the media, bloggers, newsgroups, and ranking agencies to share their unbiased opinions:

- Focus on influencers and critics in a community—their speech, both online and off, can create momentum and buzz for your product.

- Alternatively, subscribe to David Sifry's "magic middle" theory, and focus on getting mid-tier bloggers to write about your organization, hopefully spurring lots of online conversation.

- Community events and targeted pitches to traditional media also generate public awareness.

Though the organization is not paying for advertising in this model, in a traditional sense, it should do everything possible to support it through customer service programs, smart public relations efforts, intelligent content marketing efforts, and more. The marketing round should not just hope that word of mouth takes off; it should optimize the avenues for it.

This is the Groundswell, as discussed in concept by Charlene Li and Josh Bernoff in their *New York Times* bestseller of the same name. *The Groundswell* examined online grass-roots actions, but such efforts occur just as frequently offline. A synergy between the two is ideal—as evidenced by the 2008 Obama and GOP 2010 midterm campaigns.

Whatever method you choose, a successful word-of-mouth campaign requires time, patience, and constant effort. The market must have a real need or desire for the product or service. And even then, overnight successes are rare. Usually it takes years, so prepare to commit substantial human resources to supporting and maintaining the campaign.

Tom's of Maine, a personal-hygiene company, is a great example of word-of-mouth marketing. In 1970, Tom and Kate Chappell founded the company with a $5,000 loan. They wanted natural products for their children—when they couldn't find them, they decided to produce them.

In 1975, Tom's of Maine created its first successful product, a natural toothpaste. In 1978, the company introduced a "natural" fluoride toothpaste, which soon eclipsed its original formula. By 1982, the company showed annual revenues of $2 million—growth achieved through word of mouth among members of the natural-foods movement in the Northeast United States.

The revenue growth landed the company on the radar of CVS, and Tom's booked significant distribution contracts with the drugstore chain. Tom's toothpaste showed up on shelves on both U.S. coasts. Finally, the start-up broke with its word-of-mouth tradition and launched a $1.3 million advertising campaign in 1989 to market its products in the South and Middle America. The brand carried, and Tom's became the nation's de facto natural toothpaste. In 2006, Procter & Gamble bought a controlling interest in the company for $100 million.

Flanking Techniques

"Left and Right attitudes should be used if there is an obstruction overhead or to one side," Musashi said.

The middle, top, and bottom approaches are common in traditional advertising, social media, public relations, networking, and direct marketing disciplines. But what if there is no loyal customer base? What if media engagement is difficult or negative? What if regulations bar your organization from talking proactively? What if there's no time or means to use a direct approach?

When faced with such obstructions, a communications effort must employ flanking techniques such as advertising, content marketing, or search engine optimization (SEO) as primary tools. In 2010, when BP's first campaign to communicate its efforts to clean up the Deepwater Horizon oil spill failed (foundered by ethics issues and fear of lawsuits), the oil giant resorted to advertising and SEO placement to combat negative publicity.

That failed, too, in large part because the BP messages didn't match contrarian reports from the media and bloggers. Regardless of the outcome of BP's efforts, its flanking approach was chosen because of the magnitude of obstructions the company faced in getting its message across.

Another example of a troubled company deploying flanking tactics is Chrysler's rebranding of the Sebring as the Chrysler 200 in a 2011 Super Bowl ad. Chrysler was considered the U.S. automobile company most likely to collapse. It was bankrupt and had taken government bailout money as part of the U.S. government's attempts to prevent an economic depression in 2008 and 2009.

While Ford and GM had made strides to restore their images, Chrysler had been relatively silent until its incredibly gritty and attractive 2011 Super Bowl ad. And that ad needed to be something special—no traditional ad campaign would make customers believe Chrysler had a new and improved product.

Wieden + Kennedy was brought onboard to produce an unusual, two-minute spot featuring rapper Eminem. The voice-over invoked the harsh economic reality of the recession and trumpeted the character of economically torn Detroit. But it rejected the contemporary media image of Detroit, and therefore its image of Chrysler. It described the fire of adversity, and

Eminem introduced the Chrysler 200: "This is the Motor City, and this is what we do." The "Imported from Detroit" slogan spoke to an American audience that understood the trials of economic hardship, and the resiliency of the ad gave people hope. Chrysler had the runaway advertising hit of the Super Bowl.

The company made the most of it. By summer 2011, monthly sales figures for the 200 had risen from the 6,000s and 7,000s to more than 10,000 units. And in 2011, Chrysler saw some of its best sales months since 2007.

Weigh the Whole Market Situation

All four of the directional approaches work best when they are integrated into a holistic campaign, but invariably one technique is primary. The more sophisticated a program is, the more likely it is to deploy multiple approaches. For example, Apple may advertise about its newest iPhone, but it will also use word of mouth and direct marketing through email to excite its loyal customers.

Weighing the strategies in the context of tactical strengths, market situations, customer opinions for and against the brand, and the real value of your offering all drive the marketing round's decision about approach. Sometimes the avenue is obvious. Other times it is a tough decision, a choice an executive has to make from several possible approaches. This is where weighing the whole market situation makes a big difference—when the marketing round needs to employ the market research discussed in Chapter 3, "Understand Stakeholders and the Competitive Landscape," to best inform the final decision maker.

Read the Tea Leaves

"Your attitude should be large or small according to the situation," Musashi wrote. That is the heart of marketing strategically in the round. The situation—the particular immediate needs and the desired outcomes—should dictate the approach and tactics your marketing team takes.

A successful strategy depends on the entire team's ability to assess a particular situation and evaluate the research available. The marketing round is likely to have a familiarity with focus groups in advertising or public relations, with market research studies, with results of listening online or with competitive research in all fields. This information paints a picture of the market landscape and its attitudes and opportunities, as well as revealing any competitors' actions. It should reveal paths toward your objectives, and the marketing round should see which efforts are most likely to be successful given the resources at hand.

Ultimately, marketing communications between organizations and their stakeholders is about building bridges and relationships. Because many companies approach their marketing from aggressive messaging positions, there's a gap between their organizations and their people.

Smart organizations understand they need to cross this gap, they need to build a bridge for customers/donors/volunteers to create successful, loyal customers who not only buy products and services, but also advocate for the brand. To fill the gap, they bring in the ombudsman.

The concept of PR serving as an ombudsman goes back several decades. The PR person acts as a trusted intermediary between an organization and the world at large. In more recent years, customer service and online community managers have filled this role.

Today, the marketing hub should assume this mantle and look for the gaps between your organization and its stakeholders. By bridging those gaps, by resolving customer needs with strong offerings and savvy messaging, the marketing hub can help your company rise above the noise.

An example is authors' movement toward self-publishing, a result of the publishing industry's creating a massive gap between its market practices and authors and readers. Seth Godin's Domino Project seeks to bridge that gap with a new means of self-publishing. It claims to be "reinventing what it means to be a publisher, and along the way, spreading ideas we're proud to spread." One of the core beliefs is "ideas for our readers, not more readers for our ideas."

Godin uses a variety of media to promote his effort, including online media, distribution, special promotions with his partner Amazon.com, events, and a street team of individuals who use their grass-roots networks to support the effort. So far, Domino has generated significant interest.

However, like the traditional publishing industry it criticizes, the Domino Project takes only select, high-quality ideas. Domino critics charge that it selects authors the same way the traditional publishers do—seeking out voices that have the biggest marketing reach as opposed to those that have the best ideas. If the Domino Project's product doesn't match its brand promise, it may soon find itself regarded as just another publisher.

Consider More Than One Tactic

When faced with choosing an approach or a series of coordinated approaches, it is very easy for an organization to play to its existing strengths. If it has strong public relations skills, it may lean toward what it's comfortable with in its top-down campaigns—conferences and media relations. But what if advertising would be the best method for seeding the marketplace with an idea? If advertising is dismissed because it is not comfortable, because it's not a known strength, then who misses out? Your company. And your bottom line.

Overreliance on a tactical specialty is a fact of the human condition, dating back through the centuries. Fight it. Great strategic choices must stretch beyond core strengths.

Most media relations aces do not comprehend marketing. Direct marketers do not understand crowdsourcing. Advertisers rarely understand the long-term relationship work that business developers and fundraising pros participate in. Specialists are just specialists—that is why working in a collaborative roundtable environment, empowering each member of the hub to bring his strengths to bear, is essential for success.

To be a true strategist, the leader of a communications department must have firsthand knowledge of as many communications and marketing disciplines as possible. The insights drawn from all the disciplines lead to integration, as well as to the hybrid deployment of individual tactics. This creates the ability to wage campaigns using a wide variety of best practices.

Consider the social media expert. The social media purist would argue that social media is the best method to market. But companies that successfully market in that realm have learned that more is required. Inevitably, these winners weave advertising and calls to action into their blog columns and social media dashboards. This simple integration of advertising principles into social media creates opportunities for return on investment and clear measurement.

Copyblogger is a well-written, engaging blog that has mastered the use of calls to action in its right-hand column. The site sells online media components like themes, how-to marketing events, and search engine optimization through these calls to action. But the marketing doesn't begin and end with the blog. It employs email marketing and SEO as essentials to its marketing. And finally, founder and CEO Brian Clark speaks at industry events, creating relationships with online influencers and marketing minds. In essence, Copyblogger is much more than a blog; it is a well-integrated marketing machine.

Victoria's Secret is certainly a well-known brand. With more than 1,000 stores, Victoria's Secret has a significant footprint in malls everywhere. It is America's best-selling lingerie line, but it also is a marketing powerhouse.

Its in-store traffic—which, combined with its catalog sales, results in nearly $6 billion in annual sales—is the result of a refined marketing process. The aforementioned catalog is the real driver of Victoria's Secret sales. More than 400 million catalogs are mailed each year, and it is as much an entertainment magazine for men as it is a sales vehicle for women.

Then, the retailer has star models debut every year's new lingerie line in the Victoria's Secret Fashion Show, broadcast live on TV and on the Internet. The celebrity-laden event is a brand-centric broadcast phenomenon that attracts millions of viewers, and its models have gone on to individual fame—consider Tyra Banks, Stephanie Seymour, and the "Victoria's Secret Angels," who are the first brand to get their own star on the Hollywood Walk of Fame.

This two-pronged, top-down approach works for Victoria's Secret—self-manufactured star power and direct marketing power combine to form an unstoppable marketing machine.

Reacting Versus Responding to Competition

When a competitor does something that draws significant attention or garners a lot of sales, it is natural to want to react, to mimic that marketing tactic. But that may, in fact, be the worst thing to do.

Successful marketing capitalizes on your authenticity. It plays to your offering's strengths so customers will be more likely to buy. It is an expression of your culture, and its strengths and weaknesses. It is a measured response to your real and perceived competitors—a solution for stakeholders that empowers your brand to thrive regardless of competitor actions.

A knee-jerk reaction to a competitor can compromise that authenticity. That's why it is crucial for a brand's marketing leadership to respond to competitors, to explore all promotion options and approaches, rather than to blindly react. However, don't hesitate to respond in kind if that is the best option for the situation.

When the recession of 2000–01 hit, American auto manufacturers marketed no-interest financing deals. Zero-percent financing brought customers back to the dealerships in such droves that foreign automakers had no choice but to offer competitive cutbacks.

The Pepsi-and-Coke marketplace shows a different scenario.

In 2010, Pepsi launched one of the most well-known integrated marketing campaigns in recent history by allocating its Super Bowl ad budget to an online, crowdsourced social-good campaign called Pepsi Refresh. The effort revolved around social media, but it was bolstered by heavy public relations efforts and significant advertising and event sponsorship spending. It received hundreds of millions of online impressions and was a PR hit. Pepsi expanded it abroad in 2011.

Coke chose not to respond. Instead it continued marketing through its primary channels of advertising, sponsorships, PR, and some social media. Initially, it looked like Pepsi was going to run away with the throne for online marketing wizardry. There was one minor problem: Pepsi lost market share to Coke. In fact, Diet Coke superseded Pepsi as the number-two cola brand in the United States, pushing Pepsi to third place.

Some pundits dubbed Pepsi Refresh as a symbolic failure for social media marketing. But this oversimplified view fails to acknowledge several key issues: product weaknesses, the integration of PR and advertising, and the use of cause marketing as the primary thrust behind Refresh.

The market has been repeatedly told about the great success of Pepsi Refresh, but there are questions about its authenticity: the lack of a tangible theory of change, the overfocus on PR 2.0 participation metrics, and a failure to report the results of its community investments. And nonprofits that won grants have grumbled about the lack of post-award support from Pepsi.

Because Pepsi Refresh did not have a tangible theory of change—a measurable approach toward social good—no one can conclude that these outcomes are natural. They also show a lack of understanding about corporate social responsibility, authenticity, and social media. In short, now that the fanfare is over, what good did the company achieve? And, in the months after the initial push, how do people feel about their participation in Pepsi Refresh?

Customers felt that Pepsi did not refresh them; instead, they felt that Pepsi had wasted their time for marketing purposes. Pepsi's approach to reporting Refresh results has been shortsighted and has undermined some of the goodwill built through its community investments.

Meanwhile, primary competitor Coca-Cola continues to widen the gap by staying the course with its ever-present marketing and quiet corporate social responsibility initiatives. Coke took incredible strides in water stewardship, and while it doesn't market this activity, it actively communicates its strategy for resolving an issue that its products directly affect. It works with environmental partners and reports on lessons learned.

From a holistic standpoint, Coke's CSR efforts are not ideal and leave a lot to be desired. Coke doesn't communicate well about its social-good efforts, but at least the company works toward tangible goals. There's an authenticity to the Coke efforts one does not feel from Pepsi Refresh.

Coke was right to not react to Pepsi Refresh, and the market response bears out their choice. It responded, instead, by promoting its brand in a traditional, simple fashion without the complexity of a muddy cause-marketing initiative. And Coke outperformed Pepsi.

Seize First Place

After you establish first place in a market, it becomes very, very hard for a competitor to unseat you.

This is a timeless truth in marketing. Al Ries's classic books *Positioning* (with Jack Trout) and *The Origin of Brands* (with Laura Ries) revolve around unique selling propositions and branding strategies to seize first place. But while positioning and branding are crucial to a brand's capability to penetrate a cluttered marketplace, they alone do not account for stellar marketing.

Leadership is a matter of seizing a marketplace through market share. Achieving market share usually comes down to whatever makes your product or service different, whether that is quality, cost, or ease of use. Marketing that difference as unique and superior fuels demand. If word-of-mouth buzz ensues, a leadership position can begin to develop.

Marketing's role at that point is to communicate that leadership position, to expand market share to a dominant position. This is why determining the right approach is crucial to your success. Reading the tea leaves tells you where to go: Which stakeholders matter the most? How should your company approach them? Do you need to develop a unique product to meet this need? What does the company need to do to maintain leadership?

Consider Toyota's leadership in developing hybrid automobiles. This dates back to the company's decision in 2001 to launch the Prius, the second mass-produced hybrid gas/electric car in the United States. (The two-seater Honda Insight preceded it.) The Prius was a five-seat electric hybrid that also was cost-effective. The company marketed it to early adopters who would appreciate fuel economy and family-friendly vehicles that were easier on carbon emissions. Tax breaks helped early sales.

Although the Prius was not an overnight success, the company continued developing its hybrid synergy drive technology and continued to market to early adopters. The early-adopter community, typically progressive and environmentally friendly, adopted the car en masse in its second iteration in 2003—and they were fiercely loyal. By 2010, more than one million Priuses had been sold in the United States.

As fuel economy and environmental issues became more and more significant through the 2000s, Honda and Ford stepped up their competition. Toyota not only maintained its leadership, but expanded it by extending its hybrid product line to existing well-loved models like the Highlander and the Camry, as well as its Lexus line of automobiles. Word of mouth carried Toyota's reputation in the hybrid class. The Camry, Highlander, and Lexus RX 400h all sold more than 100,000 vehicles by 2010, making them the third-, fourth-, and sixth-best-selling electric hybrids in the United States for the decade. (Competitor Nissan simply licensed Toyota's hybrid technology rather than competing with it.)

Table 4.1 shows how Toyota expanded its leadership, while also expanding its product line without cannibalizing its own market share.

Table 4.1 Hybrid Electric Vehicle (HEV) Sales by Model

Vehicle	2006	2007	2008	2009	2010
Toyota Prius	106,971	181,221	158,574	139,682	140,928
Honda Insight	722	0	0	20,572	20,962
Ford Fusion				15,554	20,816
Lexus RX400h	20,161	17,291	15,200	14,464	15,119
Toyota Camry	31,341	54,477	46,272	22,887	14,587
Ford Escape	20,149	21,386	17,173	14,787	11,182
Lexus HS 250h				6,699	10,663
Toyota Highlander	31,485	22,052	19,441	11,086	7,456
Honda Civic	31,251	32,575	31,297	15,119	7,336
Nissan Altima		8,388	8,819	9,357	6,710

Toyota is a massive company, but the principle of becoming the leader in a market segment applies to small markets, too. Consider the geolocation check-in market—location-based social networking on mobile phones.

In the mid-2000s, several established telecom players such as GyPSii and Loopt tried to make geolocation a bona fide market, with limited success. A more social player Brightkite added some excitement to the marketplace, but it, too, floundered under technology issues.

Finally, Foursquare entered the scene in 2009 and took the marketplace by storm. They turned geolocation into a game, creating a system of points, leader boards, and badges. While Foursquare, too, had technical glitches, it worked better than its predecessors. By the time the scrappy New York start-up took Foursquare to SxSW in 2009, it had already executed smart product development, learning lessons from its predecessors. But it went further, outmarketing its competitors and creating a groundswell that thrust the company into the leadership position for geolocation, a position it still retains today.

Foursquare targeted the early-adopter community at the raucous SxSW interactive festival. By using Foursquare to see where the hot parties were, by creating specialized badges for the show, and by generally feeding into the social phenomenon of SxSW, Foursquare become the "it-girl" of the festival. Über blogger Robert Scoble declared 2009 as the year that "location exploded onto the scene." Online industry trade rag TechCrunch declared Foursquare the breakout hit of the event, and the geolocation leader emerged from SxSW 2009 as its industry leader.

It hasn't looked back. Bloggers and the larger social media community embraced Foursquare, cementing it into a leadership position through word of mouth—online and off—that hasn't been rattled by networks such as Gowalla and Facebook Places.

Being first was crucial for Toyota and Foursquare. It is much, much harder to unseat an established first-place company.

A rare success story in that regard is Southwest Airlines, which achieved this position not by taking on the market leaders, but by carving out a niche within the larger marketplace. Strategically targeting a specific piece of the market and becoming first in that particular segment is the best way to address established leaders. Because they can't protect their entire market share, they surrender a portion of the market to smaller, more nimble competitors. Then more and more customers migrate for better quality.

The Element of Surprise

Boring marketing is just that. A formulaic approach to a communications effort yields little interest or value to stakeholder communities. So think about the unexpected—it can be as simple as a different approach to a traditional sector.

Radiohead released a new album, *The King of Limbs*, online. The announcement came with the release of the album's first single, "Lotus Flower" on YouTube. The online release circumnavigated the traditional recording industry, which was unusual but not new. What *was* new was Radiohead's exploding the industry's traditional release pattern by offering the entire album for sale online only three days after announcing it.

The short "premarketing" ramp worked. While sales are unknown, because Radiohead owns its own distribution system, it's clear they created interest from millions of fans for the album.

Another form of surprise can involve a company's use of new and existing media for competitive advantage. If customers use multiple media—and almost of them do—then take advantage of that with new marketing and distribution methods.

One of the best examples of this strategy is Netflix. The upstart video company beat out mainstay brick-and-mortar brands like Blockbuster and Hollywood Video by using the U.S. Postal Service to deliver videos directly to customers' homes. It was cheaper than brick-and-mortar stores, it allowed customers to see more videos, and it was immensely more convenient. At first Netflix used word-of-mouth referrals and direct mail, and as the service grew it launched advertisements to market to consumers.

The tidal wave of word of mouth for Netflix completely eroded the traditional video-rental model, and it caught industry leader Blockbuster by surprise. The old guard reacted slowly, and Blockbuster lost its leadership position.

When digital video technology became widely available, Netflix repeated its first lessons and offered video streaming on demand. It deployed applications for mobile phones and tablet computers and tailored its Web site to allow customers to view movies on demand anywhere they wanted to see them. At its peak in Spring 2011, Netflix was using 10 percent of U.S. consumer bandwidth requests.

However, the company increased prices and lost some of its customer base; people were not happy with paying more for mail- and Internet-based on-demand services. Then Netflix split and created a brand for its mail service called Qwikster, which many dubbed a PR disaster. Because of that, they quickly turned around and tabled Qwikster, but some of the damage was already done. Still, at the time of writing, Netflix was the market leader in home video rental services, and continues to increase its quarterly revenue.

Measured Expenditure Matters

Our final Musashi piece of wisdom speaks to timing and sequencing: "If you try to beat too quickly, you will get out of time. Of course, slowness is bad. Really skillful people never get out of time, and are always deliberate, and never appear busy."

Marketers are always up against their budgets, yet their attitude seems to be to spend all of it as quickly as possible—they launch massive campaigns and tons of action, only to find themselves later in a lull. They have not evaluated the proper timing of a campaign, nor have they allowed for the evolution and maturation of the marketing process.

Procter & Gamble earned well-deserved praise for its Old Spice Guy campaign, which used a combination of multichannel marketing (movie and TV ads) and social media to make a stodgy brand new and exciting again. As the campaign launched in 2010, Old Spice reported increases in sales of its body-wash products. Nielsen indicated a 107 percent increase in sales when the campaign moved from traditional ads into social media on YouTube (also generating $2 billion in sales).

However, after the summer of 2010, the award-winning Wieden + Kennedy campaign suffered. The second iteration of the Old Spice Guy ads featured NFL ads with the likes of Ray Lewis. While they were well viewed, the shine had worn off the Old Spice Guy theme.

The next year, Old Spice deployed a challenge from new "Old Spice Guy" Fabio in a bizarre sequence of online ads and videos. The challenge garnered some attention, but realistically the ads were in a state of one-upmanship—how can Old Spice Guy ads be better or funnier than the originals?

The Old Spice Guy ad campaign suffered from poor planning and long-term sequencing. Perhaps the wild, overnight success of the original campaign took Procter & Gamble, and its agency, by surprise. The ads are still entertaining, but the rhythm has been lost. The question now is how will P&G use its Old Spice Guy to further develop its newfound market momentum over the years? Or will it allow him to become a comfortable spokesmodel for the brand?

Expending time and effort in a meaningful, purposeful way is an art. It means knowing when to communicate and understanding how long it takes to achieve a result. Sometimes this includes the art of saying, "not yet," or even saying no. Saying no can be very difficult for marketers; turning away a sale or an opportunity can be scary. However, going full speed and "redlining" a marketing effort can break a brand or an organization.

Exercises

Which Approach Is Right for My Company?

There is so much to consider when the marketing round weighs its general communication approach. Though the four primary methods—direct, top-down, groundswell, and flanking—are not solitary, invariably each company uses one as its primary method of communicating with customers and other stakeholders.

Use these questions to help your marketing round determine which of the four approaches makes the most sense for your company:

1. Do we have a strong loyal customer base that advocates for us of its own volition?

2. Based on our SWOT, where does our offering sit in context with our competitors' offerings?

3. Independent of the offering, how does our reputation as a company stand against other brands?

4. What are the normal methods for communication to our stakeholders?

5. Are there any emerging media use trends or approaches of communication that we and our competitors have yet to try?

6. Are we willing to experiment?

7. Is there any approach that would fail simply because the market would not welcome it, based on our current market position (for example, the staged media event)?

8. What are our strongest communications tools?

9. What are the financial assets we can bring to bear?

10. Can we acquire or gain access to other tools through agencies, vendors, or talent acquisition?

Sometimes determining approach is a question of elimination. By now you must be looking at one or two primary approaches. Choose the ones that seem most likely to succeed in a timely fashion with the least effort. Don't be afraid to use the remaining approaches as supporting tactics, simultaneously or in a staged manner.

Seizing First Place

When you find yourself in third or fourth place in the market, a great way to win in the competitive marketplace is to redefine it. Specifically, try to own a piece of the market rather than trying to dominate every aspect.

Consider whether you can position your company as first within a smaller, redefined product category. To this end, ask the following questions:

1. Does our offering lend itself to a new position that is unique and separate from all the other products and services, or is it competing on new features and/or processes?

2. If we carve off a piece of the market, can we be best at that particular area?

3. If we redefine the market or offer a service first, can our competition react quickly and close the gap (for example, cellphone carriers offering 4G services "first")?

4. Is it believable? Do market statistics back our claims?

5. Is it desirable? Just because we are the best at something doesn't mean that it's something people want.

6. Does being first in this redefined category support the marketing round and company's larger vision, brand, and market approach?

By now you are starting to get a feel for whether there is a strong possibility of carving out a niche within your market. If your marketing round feels bullish at this stage, it may be worth exploring a larger positioning exercise and strategy to be number one.

Surprise

To make significant gains in market share, it is essential to break out of the pack and attract more customers. Everyone wants to win a market by surprise, but how does one do that?

There are really three ways to achieve a surprise: Through a unique new offering, through a contrarian marketing approach, or by forging a new marketing method using different media. Use the following chart to determine whether this is an opportunity for you.

	Is the offering unique?	What is the customary marketing approach and positioning?	Which media are usually used?
You			
Competitor #1			
Competitor #2			
Competitor #3			

Look for areas of commonality between you and your top three competitors. If everything is the same across all four, then there is an opportunity to do something differently and achieve an element of surprise.

Surprise requires risk. Some risks are calculated and measured, and certainly your SWOT preparation and market analysis help you achieve that. Your marketing round should embark on this path knowing the risks, yet feel confident in closely analyzing the market. You are exploring opportunities to differentiate and achieve uniqueness.

5

When to Go Direct

When in doubt, go direct. The direct approach with customers is the most powerful form of marketing because it is the most likely to produce a sale, and it's the most measurable form. Further, when happy customers enjoy a product or service, they are likely to tell friends about it, creating critical word of mouth and brand reputation.

While often considered less "sexy" than other forms of marketing communication (such as public relations, social media, and paid advertising), direct marketing yields great results. It is not usually public and splashy, and it doesn't make media headlines, but direct marketing is the kind of one-to-one communication that triggers growth and snags long-term customers.

Direct marketing accounted for 54.2 percent of all ad expenditures in the United States in 2010, according to the Direct Marketing Association. That's a whopping $153 billion spend. DMA also says those efforts produced approximately $1.798 trillion in incremental sales, or the number of units sold through direct marketing in excess of the estimated sales performance without it.

Direct marketing usually assumes a relationship between your customers and the marketing round that is encompassed in a database. It's either that, or you have purchased a mailing list or email list.

Helzberg Diamonds, a jewelry chain, uses email marketing to sell its wares. It estimated its recipients were receiving competitive emails from five or six jewelry companies. To stand out, and to market its version of the personalized charm bracelet, Helzberg developed a customized email campaign that used an animated image that spelled each recipient's name using Helzberg's charm beads. (They used a filtering program that replaced any curse words or "pseudo" names with the word "friend.")

How did the email fare? Very well. The program increased sales 288 percent compared with an email selling the same product to the same list. Further, it experienced a 55 percent higher open rate and an 85 percent higher click-through rate than Helzberg's average email performance.[1]

In decades past, direct marketers sent print mailers and hoped to achieve two percent conversion rates. People came home and found lots of mail they didn't want—junk mail—but they also found select pieces from places they enjoyed shopping, such as Territory Ahead; Victoria's Secret; and B&H Photo, Video, and Pro Audio.

The email revolution of the '90s created a cheap, electronic method for contacting customers, and it changed the direct marketing industry forever. Initially doubted by marketers, email marketing quickly became the direct marketer's bread and butter.

This brought about the rise of spam—unsolicited emails that deluged consumers' inboxes. The resulting outcry made getting customers to agree to accept companies' emails, or "opt in," a crucial component of direct marketing strategies. Companies such as Groupon, Zappos, and Apple have mastered email sales.

In the late 2000s, the social media revolution brought a new and scarier form of direct marketing: the kind where customers talk back. Publicly. Messages no longer went unquestioned—companies began getting feedback in the moment, whether it was the kind they wanted or not.

Cultivating and maintaining direct marketing customer relationships using social media is time-intensive work. It requires community managers, well-integrated customer service practices, and savvy capture mechanisms on your Web site. But it is possible for your marketing round to succeed.

In the mid 2000s, Network Solutions lost ground online with new social media customers thanks to poor customer service and the resulting negative publicity. The company monitored conversations actively in 2007 and 2008 and began resolving issues directly. Network Solutions reinvigorated its domain-name business by using social media to directly communicate with potential customers and with customers who were upset.

Most recently, mobile marketing has become a hot direct marketing channel. For years, the limitations of mobile phones kept this channel quite small—limited text messaging and some experimental marketing. But the explosion of tablets and location-based smartphones has opened a new box of methods for your marketing round—including text messaging, application-based marketing, location-based alerts through services such as Foursquare, QR codes in physical locations, and mobile-based banner ads.

Mobile marketing is no longer experimental marketing. Forty-three percent of Americans had a smartphone by the end of September 2011, according to Nielsen. Is the mobile Web experience the same as the rest of the Web? Not quite, but it still commands seven percent of the overall page views on the Internet.

Further, Pew Internet says 47 percent of Americans received news on their phone in the first quarter of 2011. Almost every major Web brand has optimized its online experience to cater to this increasingly powerful media form.

Following are some other forms of direct marketing marketing rounds like to use:

- Trade shows and private events, which your marketing round uses to set up meetings and direct interactions with customers
- Telemarketing calls to prospective and existing customers
- A business developer who goes to networking events and directly interacts with prospects

- Print product catalogs
- Customer/channel to customer sales, where affiliates sell on your behalf

One example of in-person, event-based direct marketing is Tupperware, which pioneered a direct marketing strategy made famous through its in-home parties. The Tupperware sales boomed in the 1950s with the rise of "Jubilee"-style parties, in which salespeople are recognized and rewarded for recruiting and selling to the most people. The parties continue to this day, for Tupperware and myriad other companies. Avon, Amway, and Mary Kay all have built multibillion-dollar businesses using similar strategies.

Some direct marketers are very liberal with their definitions, and they include customer service, magazine inserts, and other forms of marketing. Whatever the method, the heart of direct marketing is a one-to-one communication with a potential customer where the company can make a sale.

Benefits of the Direct Approach

The purpose of direct marketing is primarily sales. There are other uses of direct marketing, which include keeping customers up-to-date on potential developments and alerting them to such issues as recalls and price increases. Also, direct marketing can be used as a means of word of mouth; for example, when a political party or campaign asks you to throw a party for like-minded friends and spread a particular message.

Each tactic has strengths and weaknesses; your marketing round needs to weigh both. Let's first look at the primary methods of direct marketing and their benefits.

Direct Mail

Direct mail usually is delivered by the post office, though it also can be conveyed through a premium delivery service such as FedEx, UPS, or DHL. An estimated 90 billion direct mail pieces are sent in the United States every year, according to the United States Postal Service (USPS). Following are some of the benefits of direct mail.

Direct mail is directly measurable, allowing your marketing round to examine response rates. Further, the use of custom URLs and electronic discount codes allows for additional precision with response rates, which can be delineated by how customized the direct mail package is. Given the advances in computer technology, it's possible to customize URLs by region and even zip codes. Many of us are already familiar with this technology, having received a direct mailer for a national retail chain featuring its local store.

Another core feature set for direct mail is that it is physical and can be held, carried, or posted somewhere. This allows customers to use it or refer to it as necessary.

Advertising executives like to use the physical aspect of direct mail and provide desirable customers "premiums" or high-end direct mail to evoke a positive response from customers. This includes incentives, prizes, free gifts, or other forms of unusual marketing that go beyond a message and an "ask."

Bulk mail rates can allow marketing companies to reach wide audiences. This is what the catalog marketing industry predicated part of its cost models on in earlier decades, and to a lesser extent today. Mail costs continue to rise, making this an increasingly difficult tactic.

Conversely, database management can allow your marketing round to engage in precision direct marketing to a narrow, focused audience. This includes customizing your direct mail so that customers' names are on it, a far better option than blanket approaches that use bulk mail towards zip codes and general areas.

Perhaps one of the greatest aspects of direct mail is that it will be seen. According to the USPS, almost all consumers check their mail each day, and 77 percent sort it upon receipt. Whether it is opened is an entirely different question.

Email

Due to lower costs and ease of design and delivery, email has surpassed direct mail as the primary form of direct marketing in the twenty-first century.

The cost of production of an email is relatively low, allowing your marketing round to deploy and test multiple messages and creative concepts. And as technology has advanced, with HTML-capable email you can embed diverse media, including audio, visual, and video content to create a more engaging user experience.

Timely marketing initiatives can occur with a simple email program. For example, inventory management can find a quick solution with daily or special deals to customers and opt-in lists via Groupon, Living Social, and others. Email response is immediate, with sales occurring within minutes and hours of sending a communication.

Electronic database marketing can allow for more than just a personalized email. It can also allow for a personalized customer landing page and sales experience. One-to-one marketing can extend to the sales process if it's well managed.

A well-cultivated email marketing list can enable different depths of interaction between your marketing round and your customers. Whether it's a periodic newsletter or a daily alert, customers can select and welcome the depth of interaction they receive.

Similarly, measurement with email allows for precise, customer-by-customer results. A company can measure not only open and click-through rates, but also what the customer does after clicking through to the site.

Finally, much of business has been predicated on physical location. With the Internet, that has changed, and a core component of online marketing is email. Email allows your marketing round to extend beyond borders to countries and customers it could not normally reach through conventional direct mail methods.

Social Media

Unlike other forms of direct marketing, social media does not lend itself to financial transactions. Social media's strengths lean toward bolstering brand loyalty through conversations, through addressing customer service issues, and by fostering word-of-mouth marketing.

You can provide value-added information to customers about products and services. This is a core aspect of content marketing and helps deliver thought leadership.

Listening provides additional insights directly from your customers. You can gain valuable insights and learn lessons about what motivates customers and their buying decisions. You can also learn about some areas where your product and service could improve and general needs that could be met with a new offering.

Your marketing round can add a personal touch to its brand image, whether that is wacky and fun or serious and responsive. This enables you to provide that critical human element that corporate marketing is often unable to convey.

An "evangelist community" of core customers can be cultivated with social media. By embracing these core stakeholders, and even empowering them to become ambassadors for the enterprise, your marketing round creates critical peer advocates. Social interactions with advocates and their peers can foster earned media impressions, both of the social media variety and on traditional mastheads.

Reputation issues caused by products and services can be directly addressed. This has a dual benefit, both satisfying the complaining customer and providing a public demonstration that your company is committed to the overall experience it offers.

Mobile

Direct marketing to a customer on a smartphone may be the most personal of direct marketing methods. People carry their mobile phones with them everywhere, making them items that are almost as irreplaceable as the wallet.

Your marketing round can benefit greatly by taking advantage of the mobile marketing revolution, one that, according to research conducted in Chuck Martin's book *The Third Screen,* increases with investment in the medium.

Mobile is a medium that lends itself to brevity. Simpler, shorter messaging and graphic design are often less consuming from a creative production standpoint.

Instant responses are attainable using SMS (texting) marketing. Text-based messaging lists have much higher return and open rates, in large part because people opt in only when they truly want updates from a company.

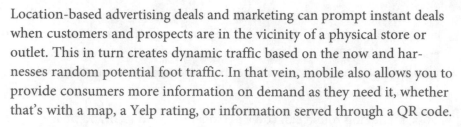

Location-based advertising deals and marketing can prompt instant deals when customers and prospects are in the vicinity of a physical store or outlet. This in turn creates dynamic traffic based on the now and harnesses random potential foot traffic. In that vein, mobile also allows you to provide consumers more information on demand as they need it, whether that's with a map, a Yelp rating, or information served through a QR code.

Applications enable you to provide a unique and customized customer experience that supersedes the quality a mobile Web page can provide. This helps you cultivate loyalists who access the company's services frequently, including on a mobile Web-enabled Web site.

Mobile payments are now easily made through secure methods such as Square, text-authorized payments, and donations. Secure networks and mobile browsing enable your storefront to move anywhere, anytime.

Events

Often considered a platform for speaking and other aspects of PR, events lend themselves to fantastic direct marketing opportunities, particularly for business-to-business outreach. Attendees at trade shows, conferences, and your marketing round's customer event are often prioritized and self-selected for targeting efforts.

Meeting customers face to face is always a stronger method of marketing than colder touches such as email or direct mail. If you have the monetary and human resources to engage in this method, we highly recommend it.

An event sponsorship gives your marketing round access to an event list. Using the list, your marketing round can pre- and post-market to attendees through telemarketing, direct mail, and email communications. Your marketing round can also qualify individuals on the attendee list by company and title and set up meetings for business developers in advance of the event. Many companies won't send certain employees to a show unless they garner meetings in advance.

Trade shows and conferences offer the opportunity for exhibit space, which can attract new customers and educate current and pre-identified prospects.

Business developers can work the floor at key sessions and networking lunches and events. For important launches or a large customer base, creating and hosting your own event may be a natural course of action, allowing you to use the entire time to interact with customers and influencers. Again, key staff can invite critical business contacts to attend and work the floor at an event.

Risks of the Direct Approach

With the good comes the bad. Although all five direct marketing methods discussed previously have strengths to offer, they also have weaknesses.

Your marketing round needs to examine those: From annoying customers with unwanted communications to extraordinarily high costs, these tactics should be vetted in full.

Direct Mail

Direct mail is probably the best known of direct marketing mechanisms, and not necessarily for positive reasons. Often dubbed "junk mail," direct mail's most common final destination is the waste bin.

As costs of producing mailers and postage rates rise, direct mail has become increasingly prohibitive. Financially, the return on investment has to occur to justify the enormous expenditure.

Prohibitive costs create additional pressure to perfect the science behind direct mail. For example, a poorly selected mailing list will not generate leads, creating a lot of waste and destroying response rates.

Consumers consider it junk. So if a company consistently sends "junk" to people who don't want it, the company's brand reputation can suffer. And consumers and environmentalists increasingly see direct mail as a waste of paper and natural resources. Younger generations tend not to respond to traditional direct mail unless it has a social or fun component.

Email

Dubbed "spam" in the mid 1990s (unless you are partial to the canned meat product), unsolicited emails have come to be loathed by consumers, who resent all these messages clogging their inboxes. An estimated 85 to 90 percent of email is considered to be spam.

When people don't like receiving email, they often act. They mark an email as spam, or in the most drastic cases, report a domain as a spamming organization. The permanent listing of your domain as a spammer can trigger spam and junk mail filters, which can prevent your emails from reaching external partners and customers.

Regular spamming is illegal in the United States under the CAN-SPAM act. Under the CAN-SPAM act, your marketing must allow recipients to opt out of receiving future emails.

In some cases, recipients—particularly those who have not opted into an email program—view the emailing organization and the organization that originally sold their email address as companies that have violated their privacy.

Social Media

Social marketers have a hard time demonstrating financial return on investment. Its benefits lean toward brand reputation, customer loyalty, and earned media hits—both social and traditional. That's not to say that you can't convert with social, but your marketing round should seriously consider other media forms first if ROI is the primary goal.

The time investments—both manpower and long-term cultivation—are unattractive to businesses that need fast results. To succeed in social media, relationships need to be built within online communities. Often they have to spend months of community investment online to build enough relationship equity to start generating sales. And when the sales do come in, the value is negligible in comparison to the costs of the staff time and associated creative design costs.

Customers talk back, sometimes negatively. Your marketing round must be ready to handle adverse commentary. And message control rarely helps in such situations, so negativity requires a deft hand with an open, honest approach to conversations that most businesses are not ready to engage in.

Many social media metrics revolve around garnering attention: retweets, Likes, Pluses, follower counts, and so on. These do not equate to business results, and business results are not obvious without a well-designed measurement program.

Success in social media often depends on others advocating for you in an uncontrolled fashion. This requires your marketing round to get beyond its own accounts in activating voices and to relinquish control of the message.

Mobile

Perhaps the biggest weakness with mobile media is the empowerment it provides its end users. Almost every aspect of mobile is chosen by the user. Whether that is looking up a review on a mobile browser, downloading an application, checking into a place with a location service, sharing a location, or texting, the customer must opt in before your marketing round can engage. Other negatives include the following:

Because mobile is technology-based, older demographics have been slow to adopt smartphones and the behaviors that a smartphone can enable. iPads and tablets have been much quicker to reach market adoption.

It is estimated that one-third to one-half of mobile page views are social-network-based. This can make the medium more relational than transaction-based, according to GroundTruth, a mobile market research firm, in turn making it harder to deliver ROI.

Consumers find text-based messaging to be even more intrusive than email. Your marketing round should cultivate its own opt-in text-messaging lists and not buy them.

Applications are costly to develop, and each platform (Apple iOS, Google Android, and so on) is unique, with its own development costs. Most people don't download applications, instead preferring the mobile Web. Only loyal customers will use applications.

Events

Events have their own risks, from requiring advance preparation to hidden costs. Because they are live and in person, they require specific skills, including event management, logistical support, and good old-fashioned business development and networking.

Events are expensive. Costs include sponsorships, trade-show space, and registration fees. There also are hidden costs to attending an event, such as travel, collateral, show booth, and display costs. Without ROI, it can be hard to justify the cost of events.

Hosting your own event is even more expensive. You have to rent a facility to hold the event and cover the costs of catering, audio-visual equipment, and more.

Small companies have a hard time standing out among large competitors at industry trade shows and conferences. Further, differentiating yourself is tough, as many trade-show and event-marketing tactics have been done before.

Success at a show requires more than showing up. It involves premarketing to a qualified list of people and following up afterward to close.

Determining Your Direct Approach

Selecting a direct marketing approach can be an educated decision. It's not as simple as "that's the way we always do it," but customer demographics, budgets, and competitive differentiation can help lead you the right way.

The most obvious thing your marketing round should consider is whether your customers prefer one contact method over another. It makes no sense to use a method that is likely to produce lackluster results. For example, if your customers are middle-aged and older, and don't attend events, direct marketing at SxSW Interactive (populated by 20- and 30-somethings) doesn't make sense.

If your budget is small, premium direct mailers and a significant trade-show booth are probably not in the cards. But email and social media can be a logical choice.

In other instances, when marketing feels like an apples-to-apples comparison with the competition, using newer tactics in mobile media and on the Internet (such as Helzberg did with its interactive email mailer) can make a huge difference.

Another example of breaking out of the conventional mold is the use of direct mail to entice millennials. Square, an application that takes financial transactions from a credit card using iPads and iPhones, markets itself by offering to send customers a free Square credit card swiping device in the mail, saving them $10 (and empowering the user to make more transactions).

Following are some questions your marketing round should ask when considering direct approaches:

1. Do we have a list? Does it include physical mailing addresses, email addresses, mobile numbers, and social media user names?

2. Given how our stakeholders use media, what are the most likely ways to achieve our desired outcomes?

3. What can we afford to do? Is it enough to make a multipronged program, or can we just manage a one-off outreach?

4. What are our competitors doing? Can we differentiate from them at an event by using a different medium or adding a creative touch?

5. Are there events where we can meet our customers face to face?

The most important thing for your marketing round to remember is the objective. Based on these answers and the medium(s) they are pointing you toward, can you achieve your sales or customer service goals?

Beware of using email marketing (or any other tactic) just because everyone is doing it or because it is the hip thing to do. Make sure your direct marketing can deliver on your objectives.

Finally, a word about creative. Creativity goes a long way in direct marketing. Consider the direct mail example earlier in which we know that 77% of all mail pieces are sorted, but getting them opened is a different matter all together. The direct mail piece needs to be developed in a way that compels the recipient to open it. This includes strong copy and great graphic design—creative.

Comscore ARS recently did a study examining how important creativity is in broadcast advertising. According of the study, the biggest variable in the success is strong creative direction for the ads.

There is a reason direct marketing is often classified as a subset of advertising. Like broadcast advertising, it relies heavily on smart ideas, good looks, and compelling copy. Whatever your method of outreach, be sure to bring writers and artists in to make your effort have the best impact possible.

Build or Buy the List

At the heart of direct marketing is the list, sometimes called the house file. You need to maintain an opt-in list with customers' preferred methods of contact. If you haven't begun managing a database of contacts, now is the time.

The easiest way to begin is to start collecting email addresses on your site for newsletters or updates. This means your marketing round will need to start producing that update, at least once a month. Companies such as Blue Sky Factory and Constant Contact can help manage your email program. For the best email providers, consider a top-ten list of providers based on overall performance and customer satisfaction built by blog Top SEOS (http://www.topseos.com/rankings-of-best-email-marketing-service).

Another way to build your list is to have customers opt in to corporate communications at the point of sale. This is how companies such as Apple and Moo Cards build their lists.

Be smart about building a list. Give customers the opportunity to add their mobile phone numbers and social media profiles for updates from those channels, too. You may not have the capacity to market to them in these ways yet, but they are relatively inexpensive to add. You never know when you will need to reach a customer.

Lastly, give the customers some sort of reward for adding their contact information to the database. Consider discounts, value-added content such as market research, fun eCards or games, or raffles for free products or prizes.

If you don't have a good database, but still want to engage in direct marketing of some sort, your marketing round will have to pay to play. That means buying a list from a third-party vendor such as a media publisher, a direct marketer, or an event company.

Most quality lists have controlled access, meaning you create the communication and the seller or a third party manages distribution (electronically or through postage). Your marketing round should consider how to add respondents to your growing list, through either opt-in email or some other means.

Be very selective about how you purchase a list. The last thing most consumers want is to hear from a company out of the blue without permission. Make sure any list you buy is permission-based.

If you are purchasing a list, consider an event, which gives your marketing round the opportunity to do more than just email or use direct mail for a limited communication. Using a trade-show booth or registration-based subevent (happy hour, and so on), you can meet prospective customers directly, build a relationship, and create your own list.

Exercises

Becoming Direct

For many communicators, becoming a direct marketer is an evolution. These exercises will help you evolve and sharpen your direct marketing skills so that you can skip expensive, indirect approaches and communicate one-to-one with your customers.

Checklist of Hidden Costs

Event marketing can be one of the most powerful methods of direct marketing. At the same time, it is one of the most expensive. Following is a list of questions to ask your marketing round to consider the full range of costs associated with an event:

- How much does a sponsorship cost? What is and isn't included with the level of sponsorship (exhibit space, email or direct mail list touches, signs, and so on)?
- Do we need to purchase the event registration list to market to potential customers before the event?
- What kind of communication do we want to send? Do we have the creative development, print, and postage budgets?
- Is the event in our hometown, or do we need to travel? How much will airfare and hotels cost?
- Can we send a business developer to the event? Will he spend time before the event making appointments and justifying the cost of sending him?

- Do we have a trade-show booth and materials for the event? Do those materials and our booth decor need to be refreshed for the event?
- What kind of follow-up will we send to our new (opt-in) registrants? Does it need to be designed?

Copywriting for Direct

Direct mail is considered an advertising discipline, in large part because the copy is written for, and to, the customer. Flowery, corporate-communications-speak laden with messaging hits the waste bin faster than an Olympic sprinter reaches the finish line.

Make sure your marketing round either has the skill to write effective direct mail copy or is going to hire it done. If you have no choice but to use your own workers, and they are inexperienced, internal resources be sure to investigate resources such as C.C. Chapman and Anne Handley's *Content Rules*. Also, be sure to have an extended group of loyal customers you can test copy on.

Following is a list of exercises to vet your copy:

- Read it to your advisory board of loyal customers. Did they get it?
- Does the communication have more than one call to action? Why?
- Do you have more than three messages in the piece? If so, send it back to the editor.
- Go back to your original goal. Does this communication provide enough value to the customer to achieve that goal?
- Test the communication on ten customers. No response? Your marketing round needs to go back to the drawing board.

Endnotes

1. Adam T. Sutton, *Marketing Sherpa*, "Email Marketing: Helzberg Diamonds garners 288% sales lift with animated, personalized promo," November 22, 2011, www.marketingsherpa.com/sample. cfm?ident=32060.

6

The Top-Down Approach

As discussed in Chapter 4, "Marketing: Tools, Tactics, Sequencing, and Timing," the top-down approach is one in which media—events, media relations, some types of advertising campaigns, and well-known influencers—are used to "inform" the marketplace about new products or services.

The message comes to the marketplace from a position of authority, and the source hopes the position of media voices, celebrities, and bloggers is enough to trickle down to the community and persuade it.

Marketing your business used to be fairly simple: You'd have public relations, advertising, and direct marketing to cover all of your top-down approaches. While advertising and PR always require an element of creativity, the traditional disciplines were well established and understood. Now digital media has disrupted everything. You also have to consider bloggers, online influencers, virtual events, and social network advertising.

Couple that with the facts that information overload is a very real thing and that there is a lot of cynicism about brands, products, services, and messages from companies.

The core of the top-down approach is you've developed enough trust with your key stakeholders that dissent doesn't occur. If you haven't worked hard to develop that trust by providing valuable information and maintaining the brand promise, if you haven't developed a position of authority, a hype bubble can occur. When that happens, customers sample your product or service and find it doesn't meet the promise. That's when the brand suffers greatly, or, worse, fails altogether.

Take Comcast, for instance. It has done an admirable job creating multiple channels for key stakeholders to communicate with them. At the corporate level, it builds relationships, enhances trust, and maintains a level of communication that every company should strive toward.

But its brand promise at the highest level doesn't always trickle down to the homes that use its services. Customers still have to be home for a four-hour window that the technician may not meet. Then perhaps the technician can't fix the problem. If you've ever had to call any cable company to come to your house, you understand. It's not a Comcast problem; it's an industry problem.

Comcast, however, has put itself out there to try to change the perception of the entire industry. Its @comcastcares Twitter customer service account has become the defacto case study for companies considering how to build online response programs. It has changed the perception of its own company—it's easy to contact the corporate office and get a response—but it creates dissent at the micro level because the brand promised isn't always delivered.

To build your top-down approach, the marketing round must be completely ready. Customer service reps should be prepared to answer questions online and off, and they should be empowered to make decisions. Public relations, advertising, and marketing should already be building relationships with key stakeholders and influencers. Sales should already be working within the marketing round to integrate lead generation and nurturing with the other disciplines. And the executive team needs to be fully supportive and engaged.

You also should understand the benefits and risks of each tool in the top-down approach.

Benefits of the Top-Down Approach

The benefits of the top-down approach are many, including cost-effectiveness, brand awareness, third-party credibility, word of mouth, image building, and more.

As the marketing round prepares to plan its resources and decide on its tactics, you'll want to understand the benefits of each tool.

Events

Events can be anything from trade shows and conferences to networking events or shows you produce. The benefits are many and allow you to kill many birds with one stone.

Events provide the capability to sell one product and launch another at one time or in just a couple of days. While you're attending events, you can keep a close eye on what your competition is doing. Walk the trade-show floor, attend their cocktail party, or even show up at their social events.

There is no better place to network with industry clients and peers than at events. They allow you to have numerous in-person meetings, whether it's a big industry trade show or your local chamber of commerce networking event.

Trade shows and conferences, in particular, allow you to digest the latest industry research, learn from industry leaders, think about the marketing round while you're out of your typical office environment, and generate ideas for growth.

You'll find, in the marketing round, most of the work you do is increasing overall brand awareness. Ever considered not attending the industry trade show, only to decide if you're not there, it will be noticed? If you take advantage of the marketing round, while you're at events, your time is very well spent.

Events are a great way to generate leads if the marketing round is working to reach the attendees in many ways and qualifying the leads before going back to the office. Events were discussed for the direct approach in depth in Chapter 5, "When to Go Direct," and as a way to meet customers who may not be willing to talk to you under normal circumstances in Chapter 8, "When to Deploy Flanking Techniques."

Face-to-face engagement still is the best way to build relationships, even though technology allows us to network every day. Being able to read body language, hear inflection in tone, and even pinpoint sarcasm helps build those relationships more quickly than even daily online communication.

Events are a great place to connect with reporters in your industry. Working in the marketing round, you can support their events (if they sponsor them), advertise in their publications, conduct interviews for stories or bylined articles, and develop relationships with the people who can provide third-party credibility. And, if it's an industry event, most of the industry's reporters will be there. You can schedule interviews back-to-back and create enough PR to last long beyond the end of the event.

How many events have you attended where you receive samples or discounts for new products or services? Events provide an extremely effective way to provide samples or create trial use. Events provide an opportunity to announce what's new: new products, new services, new promotions, new employees, new branding, or anything else that is new.

Media Relations

People typically use media relations and public relations interchangeably. The truth of the matter is, media relations is only one tactic in a PR professional's arsenal.

There are many benefits of media relations, which is the backbone of most PR programs, including cost efficiencies and third-party credibility.

Because you're not buying media space or sponsoring an event, which can cost thousands, if not hundreds of thousands, of dollars, it is the most economical way to reach mass audiences. While you have time-incurred costs, they're never as high as the out-of-pocket expenses associated with advertising media and creative.

By working in the marketing round and using media relations in combination with the other disciplines, you can stimulate awareness of, and demand for, your products or services.

According to the Edelman Trust Barometer,[1] people trust articles about a company or brand 27 percent more than they trust advertising.

Because of that, media relations develops a strong and controlled image that provides third-party credibility. It's seen as an endorsement from media, which goes a lot further than any kind of paid media.

As well, it creates the perception the company is active and has a lot going on, especially when combined in the marketing round with blogger relations and influencer relations.

Public Relations

Public relations covers everything from crisis, issues, and reputation management to corporate social responsibility, events, and media relations. The benefits of a strong and effective PR program are many, especially if conducted in an ethical way.

While not a complete list of things that lead to great PR, brand awareness, corporate social responsibility, crisis planning, and word of mouth are good places to start.

Brand awareness is usually the first thing created from PR, and it's vital to your brand's success. Not only does it speak to a larger audience, but it also creates credibility among your targets. It's extremely difficult to measure, though, so make sure you're using it in tandem with some of the other approaches discussed throughout this book.

Corporate social responsibility, or community service through the business, allows for great PR, but it also shows your willingness to support the businesses and people where you work and live. While it won't immediately affect the bottom line, people are more willing to do business with those who are supportive of them and their efforts. Always remember, people buy from those they know and like. Localizing your PR efforts to the communities in which you work allows you to be known and well liked.

Crisis planning has never been as essential as it is now in our real-time world. You don't have to look far to find examples of poor crisis planning, especially when it comes to poor customer service played out online. Many companies are experiencing loud and vocal unhappy customers complaining online and not doing anything about it, which is creating a PR crisis. A solid plan prepares you for unhappy stakeholders and allows you to expect, and react to, the unexpected.

Word of mouth is likely the best way to spread information about your brand. Positive buzz can drive foot and online traffic, generate leads, and convert new customers and brand ambassadors. This is where customer service and PR begin to intersect, which is why the marketing round is so important. PR creates an effective opportunity to develop better relationships with your customers.

Advertising

Nearly everyone understands the benefits of advertising, and the marketing round will be no different. Considered a "must have" for nearly every business, advertising is the cornerstone for brand awareness and image building. While advertising is not any more important than the other top-down approaches, it is tangible and easier for people to understand the efforts behind it than some other tools.

Advertising provides the three Rs: retain, reduce, and recruit. Through advertising, you retain loyal customers, reduce lost customers, and recruit new customers.

Advertising lets people know you're in business, promotes sales, and broadens the reach to mass audiences. It also creates a word-of-mouth opportunity. Perhaps customers see an ad promoting a new product or service. They buy it and they tell five of their friends. Suddenly the cost of your ad turned into a return on investment of six purchases.

When in print, advertising has a long life span because of the pass-along phenomenon. Rarely does just one person read a newspaper or magazine. Such items are passed along to friends, family, and even strangers.

As well, businesses that continue advertising, despite the economy, have a competitive edge over businesses that do not. Kellogg's victory in the cereal wars during the Great Depression is the perfect example of this.[2]

In the late 1920s, two companies—Kellogg's and Post—dominated the market for packaged cereal. It was still a relatively new market: Ready-to-eat cereal had been around for decades, but Americans didn't see it as a real alternative to oatmeal or cream of wheat until the 1920s. So, when the Depression hit, no one knew what would happen to consumer demand. Post did the predictable thing: It reined in expenses and cut back on advertising. But Kellogg's doubled its ad budget, moved aggressively into radio advertising, and heavily pushed its new cereal, Rice Krispies. (Snap, Crackle, and Pop first appeared in the 1930s.) By 1933, even as the economy cratered, Kellogg's profits had risen almost 30 percent and it had become what it remains today: the industry's dominant player.

Because of case studies like this, advertising continues to be one of the best ways to stay top-of-mind when a buyer is making a purchase decision. When it's combined with PR, social media, point-of-sale, and direct, the touch points are many, and the buyer can think only of your brand.

Influencers

Although it's a fairly new category for the top-down approach, especially online, influencer relations can be one of the marketing round's most effective tools for building brand awareness, establishing credibility, and driving sales.

It's not a surprise that when a celebrity endorses a product, sales increase. The same is true for online influencers, whether they are on Twitter, YouTube, Facebook, or a niche community.

Typically influencers will share a customer success story, review a product, mention your company in a case study or book, write a company overview, write a blog review, or even manage a community for you.

Not only do they help increase sales, but in some cases they can drive significant traffic to your owned sites—Web sites and blogs.

They provide an inexpensive and very valuable way to test your messaging because they typically are your customer, so they know what others want or request. And, because they aren't affiliated with your company, they tend to be able to take a more strategic look at the competitive landscape because they aren't mired down in the details.

Their networks are separate from your own, so they are able to introduce your products or services to new audiences and help you generate leads. And, just as with traditional media, influencers become third-party credibility.

Risks of the Top-Down Approach

In the 1990s and early 2000s, consumers trusted third-party media nearly as much as they trusted recommendations from friends and family. As is shown in Figure 6.1, a 2009 Nielsen survey[3] found that editorial content had fallen more than 20 percent and had been replaced by online opinions and brand Web sites.

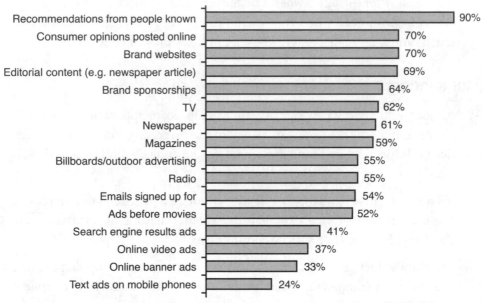

Have Some Degree of Trust* in the Following Forms of Advertising April 2009

Recommendations from people known	90%
Consumer opinions posted online	70%
Brand websites	70%
Editorial content (e.g. newspaper article)	69%
Brand sponsorships	64%
TV	62%
Newspaper	61%
Magazines	59%
Billboards/outdoor advertising	55%
Radio	55%
Emails signed up for	54%
Ads before movies	52%
Search engine results ads	41%
Online video ads	37%
Online banner ads	33%
Text ads on mobile phones	24%

Source: The Nielsen Company
*E.g. 90 percent of respondents trusted "completely" or "somewhat" recommendations from people they know

Figure 6.1   *Media is no longer the most trusted source for information.*

Because of this shift in trust, the marketing round must determine which top-down approach makes the most sense for the company's audiences and for communicating the features and benefits of your products or services.

Events

The risks of events mostly relate to the fact that the landscape has changed so much in the past few years. Trade shows used to be the place to go to do an entire year's worth of business. Now creativity in attending those same shows reigns supreme.

Attendance is down at most events, especially industry trade shows, as expense budgets are cut and people favor staying home over getting on a plane for business travel. Just like you can do at events, competitors can watch you. Some will even go so far as to send "spies" to your booth, your speaking engagement, or your break-out session, or even eavesdrop on your conversations with trade reporters.

Sometimes a decision is made to attend an event solely because you'll be missed if you're not there. That's not always the best use of scarce resources. But if you do attend, keep in mind most attendees are tired of the same old ways of getting people to your booth. The email marketing before the show, the in-booth gimmicks, and even the door hangers at every hotel room are stale. Attending an event, even if it's one you're sponsoring or putting on, requires an inordinate amount of creativity if you're going to stand out.

Some events are turning virtual, taking advantage of technology and low attendance at in-person events. But people have a tendency to multitask and not be fully present at virtual events. It's human nature, and it cuts the effectiveness of the event. Using this approach means you have to consider new and interesting ways to keep people's attention, such as recording sessions ahead of time and using the live time for questions with the presenter.

Some media outlets have stopped sending reporters or stringers to events, which ends the benefit of being able to schedule one-on-one meetings with each.

In addition, unforseen circumstances can torpedo an event: a protest, a last-minute speaker cancellation, a catering failure. Planning to handle such problems is a must, and it's a time-consuming, resource-draining must.

Media Relations

While media relations, or publicity, is a great ego stroke, it's extremely difficult to measure its worth in real dollars. There is nothing better than your friends, family, industry peers, and competitors seeing your company, brand, products, or services on the news, on the radio, or in print. But rarely is that the reason anyone buys from you.

Media relations, used alone, does not increase sales. Its lead times are extraordinarily long—up to a year in some cases—and that makes it difficult to measure its direct effect on sales and profits.

And, it's not as effective or influential (refer to Figure 6.1) as it once was. After the economy tanked in 2008, media outlets began going out of business. Many of the relationships that the PR pros in your marketing round spent years cultivating are gone. Because of that, news outlets are no longer trusted as much as word-of-mouth information or even as much as your owned media (your Web site or blog).

Public Relations

Public relations has a perception problem. The industry struggles to define what it does, and it's not tangible—you can't touch it or see it—so it's difficult to describe.

Corporate social responsibility, particularly, can be perceived as something companies do just for the good PR. Because of the bullhorn people now have with social media, customers are becoming more critical of things they believe are not done in the best interest of them. Companies can be caught without a strong crisis plan in place if something unexpected happens, creating a bigger issue than in the past if not responded to in real-time.

On the flip side of response in real-time, relying on word of mouth requires having a certain amount of transparency, giving up the perception of control, and really allowing your customers to have a say in how your business is run.

Because the industry doesn't do a good job of defining its definition or metrics, public relations becomes less tangible. Without being able to prove its effectiveness, it's typically the first to go when budgets are cut.

Advertising

Just like public relations, advertising has a perception issue that makes it difficult to find a return on investment and measure its effect on sales and profits. And, as you saw in Figure 6.1, it's the least-trusted form of media.

With the invention of DVR and today's information overload phenomenon, people skip ads entirely, rendering them useless.

The Federal Trade Commission closely monitors advertising, so every message must be backed up by facts. False advertising is punishable by large fines or (in severe cases) jail time.

Influencers

According to a new study from PayPal,[4] celebrity spokespeople are less influential in sales than an organization's community of customers, brand ambassadors, and referral network. You need to understand your biggest influencer may be the collective community of people using your product or service, and not a celebrity endorser or a blogger with a large following.

Determining whether or not an influencer will be paid is the same conversation of whether or not you need to advertise with a trade publication to get editorial coverage. Paying your influencers must be disclosed and customers may not see it as a separation of church and state. Because of this, you have to be careful about working with influencers whose agenda aligns with your own.

Taking the time to develop relationships with them will help you find the right people with whom to work. But through all of this, remember it's difficult to show a return on investment, even if it's just time spent. You'll know, intuitively, whether or not it's working, but you may not be able to show its effectiveness straight to the bottom line.

Determining Your Top-Down Approach

There isn't a scientific approach to determining your top-down tactics. Pay attention to what the industry does really well...and to what doesn't work. Also pay attention to what the industry is not doing. That will be an opportunity for you. Understand the benefits and risks for each option and test, test, test.

Annual marketing plans used to be created in the fourth quarter, and then companies were stuck with them for a year before you could measure results. But in today's digital world, you'll know as soon as a month, if not a week, that something is or isn't working. This immediacy provides a huge opportunity for testing and for combining with tools such as direct (Chapter 5), crowdsourcing (Chapter 7, "The Groundswell Approach"), or social media (Chapter 8).

Ask yourself the following questions:

1. Do you have information that is valuable and will inform your audiences?

2. Have you built a strong level of trust with your audiences?

3. Do relationships with media, influencers, and bloggers already exist?

4. Does your company already have a position of authority among the top-down influencers, with your audiences, and within the industry?

5. Are you well respected (if not well liked) among your competition?

If you answer yes to these questions, the top-down approach can be effective for you.

Too many companies want to begin using the marketing round without having built relationships or developed a level of trust with their key stakeholders. The job of the marketing round is to create, build, and maintain relationships with human beings, online and off. And that takes time. It's not a "we're launching a product next month and want everyone to know" approach. When you're dealing with people, it takes time. Make the time. Plan for the time. And get to the point where you can answer yes to the five questions posed previously.

When you can do that, it's time to begin your top-down approach.

Exercises

Determining which tools you're going to use—events, media relations, public relations, advertising, or influencer relations—is going to take some skill, some expertise, and some experimentation. The following exercises will help.

Getting to the Yes

Regarding the previous five questions, if you answered no to any of them, this exercise will help you get to the yes.

Do you have information that is valuable and will inform your audiences?

If the answer is no, take a look around. Ask the marketing round to bring collateral, sales materials, brochures, ads, news articles, blog posts, and even a printout of the Web site to your next meeting.

Spread out all the information on the conference room table and, using a red pen, begin removing the French—the "we, we, we." Also excise the "us," and any other self-focused terms.

Then, as a team, take an hour or two and think about what content you can create that will be valuable to your stakeholders and also will be searchable. To generate topics, consider questions people ask during sales meetings, challenges your products or services have, pricing, and the "versus" questions.

The questions people ask during sales meetings are going to be the easiest to answer. Ask everyone to write down five questions they're asked all the time. Even if they don't go to sales meetings, everyone talks to customers. Write down at least five questions for everyone in the marketing round.

Creating content around challenges or issues is uncomfortable, but it's that kind of content that people search for when they're online. Do you want to confront the challenges or issues head-on? Or would you rather your competitors handle that for you?

Marcus Sheridan, co-founder of River Pools and Spas and blogger at The Sales Lion, is a big proponent of putting your pricing on your Web site. It's always the first question people ask, and it helps to determine whether or not the person is a potential new customer. If you're uncomfortable with pricing on your site, think about ways that can qualify potential customers by using minimums or packages.

And the last topic for the meeting should be the "versus" content, meaning this versus that. For instance, using the cloud versus having a server, or public relations versus marketing. This also should take into account what people search when they're looking to do business with a company in your industry.

By the end of this meeting, you'll have a new focus for all of your materials, as well as new content to use in your Web properties.

Spend the next 30 days revising your new and existing materials to have a customer-centric tone. This will make your existing content newly valuable and informative to anyone who comes across it.

Have you built a strong level of trust with your audiences?

Have you ever been told, "Get XYZ publication to cover this!" Or, "See whether XYZ influencer will talk about our product!" Or, "Get an ad placed by Sunday!"

The joke always is that you can get immediate coverage, no matter who you know, if you've committed a crime. But barring actions that will land you behind bars, none of those things is possible without some lead time and without building relationships. Remember that you're working with human beings—especially when it's media, bloggers, or influencers—and you have to build in time to do that.

The best way to develop those relationships is to read and comment on the content they're creating. It's not a task you can shortcut, and it takes a lot of time. But if you scratch their backs, eventually they'll scratch yours.

During your marketing-round meeting, develop a list of top-priority media outlets, influencers, and bloggers. Divide the list among the team so that each is responsible for reading and commenting on the content that each of those people creates. (And make sure that they're empowered to comment on behalf of the company.)

This approach works with traditional media, as well as new media. Because many journalists are now covering more than one beat, they are reading the comments people post on their stories. They're then turning those people, at least those who write something professional and wise, into sources for future stories.

Do relationships with media, influencers, and bloggers already exist?

It's not enough to say you have something new and to expect media, influencers, and bloggers are going to be excited to write a story for you.

Media relations, as it's known in the PR world, is about relationships. If you've ever sat in an IABC or PRSA meeting where journalists are speaking or on a panel, you've heard them say over and over again, "Read what

I write. Get to know me. Know who my readers are. Don't send me a story that doesn't fit those criteria."

It's hard work, but you're building relationships with human beings. If you actually take the time to read what they write, get to know them, and understand their audiences, you will be successful in gaining their attention...and eventually a blog post, story, or news segment.

There are tools to help you lay the groundwork: Cision, Vocus, Technorati, and even Google blog search help you develop a list of people you want to target.

But then it's up to you to prioritize that list. Start with the top ten and work your way down the list. Get to know the journalists or bloggers. Comment on their articles or blog posts. Engage with their communities.

It takes time, but it works.

Does the company already have a position of authority among the top-down influencers, with your audiences, and within the industry?

The term "thought leadership" is overplayed, but that's the type of position you need to create through the marketing round.

You can do this effectively through owned media, which is the type of content you're creating by "getting to the yes" in the first question about valuable information.

The more valuable your content, the more people want to share it with their networks. And the more they share, the higher your position of authority soars.

Are you well respected (if not well liked) among your competition?

Many business leaders are afraid to become active with top-down approaches because they don't want competitors to know what they're doing. But as you work with influencers and develop your position of authority, competitors begin to look at you as the industry leader.

There is always going to be proprietary information you won't use in your top-down approaches. But you can demonstrate how people inside your company think without giving away the secret sauce.

After you've gotten to the yes, it will be easier to decide which top-down approaches to use. By getting to the yes, you'll have built a foundation for each. Deciding where to go next will be easy, because the choice will be based on the relationships you have, what's happening within the industry, and your particular business strategies.

Endnotes

1. www.edelman.com/trust/2010/.

2. www.spinsucks.com/spin/what-kelloggs-and-the-great-depression-can-teach-you-about-pr-and-marketing/.

3. http://blog.nielsen.com/nielsenwire/consumer/global-advertising-consumers-trust-real-friends-and-virtual-strangers-the-most/.

4. http://geofflivingston.com/2011/11/03/paypal-research-shows-strength-of-community-trumps-popularity/.

7

The Groundswell
Approach

Your company, and therefore your marketing round, is likely working with a tight budget, which is going to require you to be very strategic about how you choose your tactics.

Some of the most powerful groundswell tools are brand monitoring, word of mouth, brand ambassadors, public and private communities, owned content, user-generated content, crowdsourcing, and social media.

The marketing department can foster the relationships necessary in the groundswell by seeding conversations that help foster forward motion and boost sales.

But it's increasingly important those in the marketing round work together. Customer service, public relations, community managers, and sales must work so the left and right hands know what the other is doing and provide a unified front to external stakeholders. Though you aren't paying high out-of-pocket expenses for this approach, time from everyone on the team is necessary.

While most of the tools used in the groundswell approach are free, the time and effort associated with implementing them are not. Realistically, however, time and effort are easier to fit into a tight budget than money for a media buy, for collateral printing, or for the redesign of your Web site.

Benefits of the Groundswell Approach

Traditionally, marketing is accustomed to shouting at its customers and prospects and then listening for the echo.

That approach is great for the top end of the funnel (see Figure 7.1), where awareness is being built. But it doesn't allow you to reach in the middle of the funnel, where consideration is built before action (conversion) takes place.

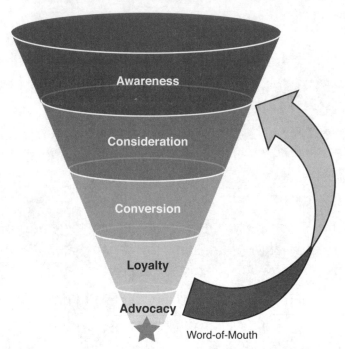

Figure 7.1   *The groundswell marketing funnel. Source: adamhcohen.com*

To successfully initiate a groundswell, the focus must be on the consideration part of the marketing funnel. If the marketing round isn't already using the groundswell, a new skill will need to be developed: listening.

What you do with the information you receive while listening is just as important as any effort you put forth.

The groundswell involves people, comments, and feedback—probably more feedback than you're comfortable receiving. It's going to get messy. Tempers are going to flare. Feelings will be hurt. You're going to feel a loss of control. The marketing round will need to develop a thick skin to really listen and make a change.

Are you ready?

Brand Monitoring

Your brand is what your customers say it is. While you define and manage the brand, if it doesn't match the customer's experience, they will determine your brand for you. In the groundswell is where the customers communicate with one another, so they're the ones deciding what they like, what they don't like, and what you need to add or change.

Monitoring what customers have to say is imperative. Listening to their feedback is critical. They're not "nice to haves." They're necessities.

A foundation for any monitoring program is Google Alerts. Every company should use this free tool—it sends emails to a designated person every time your company, brand, product, or service is mentioned online.

While Google alerts work really well as you begin your monitoring program, as the marketing round becomes more sophisticated and you're using more and more of the groundswell, you'll need to graduate to a paid monitoring service. Those services include Spiral16, Sysomos, or Radian6.

One of the first steps to brand monitoring is listening.

Listening, not just monitoring, but really paying attention to what current and past customers, competitors, and the industry have to say gives you a huge amount of market research you would have had to pay hundreds of thousands of dollars for ten years ago. You can ask questions, get feedback, and even test new product or service ideas if you are monitoring conversations correctly.

But listening takes skill. It takes thick skin. It requires someone who won't get his feelings hurt or get defensive. Someone in your marketing round should be responsible not only for listening, but also for keeping everyone else updated on what he learns. It's a real-time, everyday job.

After you set the foundation, you can begin to listen to what your key stakeholders are saying to one another. Although they may intuitively know you're listening, they're as honest as if you were not there. Consider the many Facebook pages that are created by both wild fans and critics of brands. Those companies don't own or control those pages, but they have the opportunity to listen, monitor, and even participate in the conversations.

Of course, creating the groundswell foundation is scary. Customers, detractors, and even loyalists will have negative things to say about you. It's human nature. But the way in which you build your program to incorporate feedback will be the difference between negative and positive experiences.

Because of this fear, you may have a hard time gaining approval from the executives for brand monitoring or listening. If that's the case, call it market research, surveys, or focus groups. These are terms they're accustomed to hearing...and including in their budgets. Rather, though, than spend three evenings behind one-way glass listening to what 100 or so past, current, and future customers have to say about your brand, you can monitor 24/7 what thousands have to say. The conversations happen in real-time and provide constant feedback—feedback you can use to improve your products, services, or even operations.

Monitoring the groundswell reveals new insights daily, if not multiple times each day. Stakeholders are voicing their opinions on the social networks, in blogs and comments, on discussion boards, and inside apps such as Yelp, Foursquare, and TripAdvisor.

As you monitor, begin to segment people by sentiment (happy, angry, excited), loyalty, positive versus negative, and more. While these are not the things you'll use to measure your results, they can give you insight into whether the company is delivering on what it thinks is its brand promise. It helps you discover what your brand truly stands for outside of your four walls.

But it doesn't have to be all scary. With brand monitoring, you can quickly discover rogue employees or a brewing crisis.

Take Domino's, for instance. It discovered some employees had posted a YouTube video of themselves sneezing and spitting in customers' food, and it responded in kind—it posted a YouTube video apology from then-CEO David Brandon. This allowed Domino's to manage a crisis on the site where people were going to see the former employees' video. And Domino's discovered it from a loyal customer who found the original video on YouTube.

As well, brand monitoring lets you generate product and marketing ideas by listening to what people want. Thinking about launching a new product or service? Seed some conversations in the groundswell and listen to what people have to say. This gives you invaluable information for proceeding.

Word-of-Mouth Marketing

According to the Word-of-Mouth Marketing Association (WOMMA),[1] word of mouth is "the act of consumers providing information to other consumers."

It used to be if a person loved your product or service, she would tell a handful of people. Now people can tell hundreds or thousands of other people because of the networks they've built online.

Keeping that in mind, WOMMA further defines word-of-mouth marketing as "giving people a reason to talk about your products and services, and making it easier for that conversation to take place. It is the art and science of building active, mutually beneficial consumer-to-consumer and consumer-to-marketer communications."

What this means is you must energize your most loyal customers. Word-of-mouth marketing will help you find those committed customers and turn them into brand ambassadors. It will also help you find your critics and, by listening and making changes, turn them into ambassadors.

While it is something that can't be forced or controlled, word-of-mouth-marketing can be seeded with smart strategy and a little elbow grease. It's tailor-made for the online world, where messages, good stories, and fun campaigns can go viral. Though it is very powerful offline, it's even stronger now because of customers' social networks.

And customers' social networks are what make it customer-centric. An April 2011, the "S-Net: The Impact of Social Media" study by ROI

Research[2] found 60 percent of U.S. social network users were at least somewhat likely to take action when a friend posted something about a product, service, company, or brand. This is word of mouth.

It's self-reinforcing: If you hear a message from one person you trust, you think about it. But when you hear the same thing from five or ten people, you buy. No longer, however, does that message have to be from your neighbor, your family, or a high school friend. The people we trust are those we met on Twitter, on Facebook, via LinkedIn, or on YouTube.

And, through brand monitoring, listening, and word of mouth, you will identify the opinion leaders in your industry and among your customers.

Brand Ambassadors

A brand ambassador program can be sophisticated and gigantic. Or it can be simple. Take, for instance, the Babybel brand from The Laughing Cow. Its PR firm, Porter Novelli, was challenged to find influencers who represented the four areas that are important to its target consumers: health, nutrition, fitness, and lifestyle.

It monitored the Web to discover not only who was talking about Babybel, but who had the most influence in each of those four areas. When it found them, it invited them to become brand ambassadors, who now write for The Laughing Cow blog,[3] tweet, Facebook, and generally talk about Babybel for a few thousand dollars a year.

This creates valuable content in an inexpensive and easy way, and it allows the brand ambassadors to do what they do best: encourage their networks to buy Babybel.

As Babybel learned, brand ambassadors help increase sales because people buy from people they like and trust, even if they're only acquainted online. When your brand ambassadors speak or write, your prospective customers buy. And your brand ambassadors don't have to be celebrities with big names.

Celebrity spokespeople are the brand ambassadors of old. But your brand ambassador might be a blogger with 200 extremely engaged readers or someone who has 20,000 Twitter followers. The job of the marketing round is to find the people who are highly influential in the industry and among your customers. It may not be the person with the high Klout score or an

Ad Age top 100 blogger. Pay attention less to the numbers and more to what readers, followers, or fans do when these people speak.

But brand ambassadors don't have to be someone from the outside. After all, employees are the best advocates for their companies. While they're paid to represent the company, they best represent the culture, the values, and the vision. Zappos, Lowe's, Southwest Airlines, Ford, Domino's, Bank of America, Comcast, General Electric, and Verizon all have used employees in broadcast and print advertising, bylined articles in print publications, blogging, commenting, and social networks.

No matter how you create a brand ambassador program, you can rest assured it will create a community of people who are passionate and care about your brand.

Communities

This is not the Field of Dreams. If you build it, they will not come.

So you want to be sure there isn't already an active community that supports your brand. Do your homework.

It's going to be easier participating in an existing community than building your own. But the return-on-investment will be greater if you build your own and it takes off. This is where the marketing round really shines because it allows you to work together to determine how the community should work. Your sales and customer service teams will know who your brand ambassadors are. Use those people to help you design and develop the community.

A community means your customers and prospective customers are talking to one another, even if you're not igniting the conversation. If a community does not already exist, it will take you some time to build one of people who trust you, trust you'll leave them alone to have conversations, and trust one another. But after that trust is built, you can feed certain topics for discussion, such as feedback on something new you're launching, and then let the talk amongst themselves, while you monitor and listen.

With a community you can start small. Choose one topic, one product, or one service and build around that. Eventually, you may support multiple communities, but starting small helps you determine whether a community will build and whether you'll be able to generate activity.

Human beings are attracted to activity. If they see a blog post has been retweeted hundreds of times, they're more likely to read, comment, and share it instead of one that has been retweeted a handful of times. Building a community allows you to create activity that is attractive to your audiences.

A goal of increased activity gives you a reason to let people compete and build their reputations within your community. Livefyre, the blog commenting system, assigns points for every comment left. So it's easy to tell who is most active in blog comments. A reputation system is a nice way to reward your active participants.

Using a community presents an opportunity to learn from your customers. They are the ones using your products or services, and they are more than willing to tell you what works, what doesn't work, and which features to add. All you have to do is be willing to listen.

Content Marketing

In the past, you had paid media (advertising) and earned media (public relations). Now the content you create for your key stakeholders is owned. You don't have to rely solely on a big media buy and third-party influencers to talk about your product or service. You can create that conversation by developing valuable resources based on your intellectual property.

Some may argue their intellectual property is what sets them apart, so they're not keen on giving it away. In owned media, however, you can inform your customers and put a face to the brand without giving away your secret sauce. If done in an educational and informative way, people will want to share your content, which feeds into word of mouth and community building.

There are several examples of owned content: White papers, blogs, email marketing, videos, and podcasts are a few.

As you develop your owned content, you begin to be perceived as an expert (assuming, of course, it's valuable and not full of sales speak). Even your competition begins to see you as an expert and tries to emulate you. You build a strong leadership position, with the help of your key stakeholders *and* your competition.

It also helps you begin to build trust. People buy from people they like and trust. Owned content allows you to develop that one-on-one, human interaction in a very effective way.

But, most importantly, it allows the marketing round to truly integrate and work together as one.

People don't choose to watch commercials, but they will watch, and share, videos that are clever and interesting. Think about the types of videos that have gone viral—Will It Blend is a great example—and the attributes they have that you can steal.

Blogs, in particular, help companies solve complex problems and make decision making easy in the middle of the marketing funnel. They also help reassure a purchase decision at the beginning, in the middle, and at the end.

It showcases all the talents of a truly integrated marketing round. Marketing uses email and direct to let people know where they can find your content. Advertising uses the URLs in their ads. Public relations uses the newswires and enhances search engine optimization. And so on.

User-Generated Content

One of the most effective ways to create and produce new content is to have your audiences create it. In some cases, they already are doing so by blogging, using tools such as Pinterest, Tumblr, and Instagram, or producing videos.

Now you have the opportunity to ask whether you can repurpose that content. Ragan does a nice job of this. For both PR Daily and Ragan.com, Roula Amire and Michael Sebastian scour the Web for blog posts about PR. They then ask the author, typically via email, whether they can repurpose the content on one of their sites.

This allows them accessibility to the smartest minds in the industry, but also to new content they don't have to produce themselves.

Amazon also does this well. While the site has numerous administrators, the users are the ones who provide the ratings, reviews, and recommendations. Without customers' input the site wouldn't be as robust, or as trustworthy, as it has become.

Some of the world's largest websites have user-generated content. The Huffington Post is another example of working with experts who provide their content in exchange for visibility and credibility.

But you don't have to take these same approaches. You can consider conducting interviews, using social Q&A sites (such as LinkedIn or Quora), or holding contests.

However you decide to approach user-generated content, it will save you significant time and money while giving you access to content you couldn't produce as effectively, efficiently, or creatively on your own.

Crowdsourcing

Crowdsourcing is asking your customers, prospects, and even competitors to provide you with ideas. If you've built your community, you support your brand ambassadors, and you listen to their feedback, crowdsourcing allows you to take your marketing round goals to the next level.

If you have customers, they can help you through crowdsourcing, if you listen, really listen, to the good, the bad, and the ugly. Listening to all the feedback allows you to crowdsource in a way that most companies aren't yet comfortable doing.

Embracing your customers and their ideas takes some skill and a lot of humility. You're working with human beings and we all like to have our egos stroked. The more ego stroking you do, the better ideas you'll gain, which makes you more innovative than your competition.

Though the restaurant is now closed, OM in Minneapolis did a phenomenal job with crowdsourcing before it opened.

Jennifer Lueck, the sales and marketing manager at the time, used Facebook and Twitter to create a community because she didn't have the time or resources to build a company-owned platform.

Knowing one of her biggest challenges was that the owner chef was from New York City, she wanted to get Minneapolis residents involved in building the restaurant early on.

She spent the first six months finding people to follow on Twitter, by using tools such as Twitter search and WeFollow. She engaged them and had conversations about food and the restaurant scene in the Twin Cities. Eventually, those same people also became Facebook fans.

When it came time to make decisions about things such as flatware, linens, and the paint color on the interior walls, she took those decisions to her community.

When the restaurant opened, it was a huge success, with reservations as long as six months out, because people felt as though they had ownership in its success. Their issue in the end, though, was not in how they crowd-sourced, but in how they fell victim to the economy.

Think about how the marketing round can achieve a similar success. It allows you to move the company forward in a positive way because the people who buy from you are intimately involved in product development and innovation.

It allows you to respond more quickly. If you crowdsource, you need to be prepared to act on the ideas. The more you act on the ideas (or give a very valid reason for not doing so), the more respected you are. The more respected you are, the more active your community. And the more active your community, the better ideas you gain through crowdsourcing.

It accelerates innovation because you're having a conversation with your customers, asking the right questions, listening, and doing some ego stroking. The balance among all four of those things allows you to use their knowledge to help you.

Social Media

Social media: Likely you're using it effectively, dabbling in it, or avoiding it even though your CEO has demanded you "get a Facebook page."

The biggest issue with social media is people forget to be social. Instead, they use it as another tool to yell at their customers and prospects, using the same messages they always use, and then they wonder why it's not working.

For instance, you don't go to a networking event, meet someone for the first time, and say: "We have this new product we're launching and, based on the shoes you're wearing, we think you'd be perfect for it. Would you like to buy it?"

Social media is about conversation, networking, and engagement. Find something you have in common and strike up a conversation. Begin to network. See whether there is a reason to work together. And then proceed.

Remember to be *social.*

There is great debate about whether or not social media can be measured. People are constantly asking, "What's the ROI?"

By itself, social media is very difficult to measure. But that's why you're using it as *one* tactic in your marketing round. Because, when used as part of a larger strategy, it can—and should—be measured (which is discussed in Chapter 11, "Measure Results to Dollars and Cents").

But, as part of your tactical planning, consider how it affects all of the things already discussed in this chapter.

It develops word of mouth so people are talking to one another about you, which provides a trustworthy and relevant conversation without your having to be involved.

It allows you to get the message out quickly and to more people. Social media means you have a potential global audience of thousands or millions to expose to your brands, messages, and thinking.

It improves branding with global exposure. It allows others to put forth your brand with one click of the mouse, extending your network beyond your own.

It's another tool David can use to beat Goliath—it provides resources and efficiencies most small companies didn't have before social media.

It exposes you to different ideas, thinking, and theories. Wisdom that once took years to gain can now be garnered fairly quickly if you're willing to invest the time to research, read, and act upon it.

While your company may not benefit from Twitter or Facebook, it's likely it will benefit from YouTube and Google+. Or vice versa. Social media isn't just for consumer brands anymore. As part of your marketing round, it touches nearly every tactic you execute, online and off.

Risks of the Groundswell Approach

In today's digital age, it would be silly to ignore the groundswell, even if your organization is business-to-business or a not-for-profit. That said, there are some risks for each of the groundswell tactics that you need to consider as you embark on integrating some or all of them into the marketing round's arsenal.

Brand Monitoring

Cynics will tell you it's not necessary to listen to the groundswell, that what the marketing round creates through products, services, and messages is what the customer is going to get.

Earlier in this chapter, you learned part of brand monitoring and listening is to develop a thick skin .You may not like what the groundswell has to say. You're going to hear things you never considered or don't want to hear. You're going to get defensive. You're going to mumble, "They just don't get it."

It will be hard to get all your marketing round to really listen to what's being said, and to decide how to respond.

It will be hard.

Word-of-Mouth Marketing

Word of mouth cannot be controlled, and people will say negative things about you, your brand, your products, or your services. It used to be that if someone was unhappy, he'd tell a handful of people. Now dissatisfied customers can write reviews or tweet or create videos that allow the message to be amplified.

It cannot be controlled, and it is inconsistent. One week you'll feel as though the entire world is talking about your brand, and the next you'll be able to hear crickets chirping.

People will say negative things about you, and those things will be amplified and spread very quickly. (You may regain the advantage if you respond appropriately.)

Your reputation is on the line all the time, which means the marketing round needs to work hard and be completely transparent. If you screw up or someone is unhappy, apologize and fix it. Don't get defensive and point fingers.

Transparency is crucial when using word-of-mouth marketing. This is a scary thing for most executives to use, and most don't want to empower their teams to make real-time and immediate decisions. If the marketing round does not have this buy-in, word of mouth won't work.

Brand Ambassadors

If you pay some of your brand ambassadors, especially if they're helping you create content, the risk is they won't be seen as credible because they're paid spokespeople. Make sure they are transparent when discussing their work with you to help mitigate that.

They can (and sometimes do) turn on you. If your brand ambassadors have a large following and are very vocal, they can create quite a stir and even hurt sales.

Brand ambassadors can, and do, move on. Just like keeping your sales pipeline full so you aren't caught without a way to grow, keeping your brand ambassadors evolving is important.

Every one of you in the marketing round is accustomed to controlling the message and talking only about the features and benefits you determine to be most important. Brand ambassadors, however, determine what is most important to them, and it might very well not be on your radar or at the very bottom of the list. Some reprioritization may be necessary.

Communities

Developing a community that works to build awareness, create credibility, and help you compete, and that is engaged, is a lot of hard work. It takes time and patience every single day. Your community cannot be ignored. It needs to be nurtured. It needs to be stroked. Without those things, it will not grow.

It takes a lot of ego stroking. People want to be liked, and they want to feel smart. As part of your community, they want both of those things and they want to know you're listening and responding. If it doesn't happen, there will be trouble.

You may build it and they won't come. If no one is participating, the marketing round has to figure out how to spread the message, how to build a community, and how to get people engaged.

The community needs consistent activity. It could be several times a day on the social networks, blog posts multiple times each week, or a private Ning group. It's difficult to build, and it's difficult to maintain, let alone grow. But participation on your part is crucial.

It can go rogue. You cannot predict what the community will respond to, nor can you control where they take the conversation. If you take the tact of deleting comments or moderating conversation, you will have a crisis on your hands you're not expecting. Be prepared for every scenario, even if you think it's a very low possibility something could go wrong.

Content Marketing

Owned content, if done well, is one of the most effective tools the marketing round can use. The problem is it is extremely time- and labor-intensive. Once you decide to go down the owned content road, and you're providing extremely valuable content, it grows fairly quickly into one or more full-time jobs.

Owned content becomes very personal because the marketing round is extremely passionate about it. It cannot be crammed down anyone's throat, and what people react to may not be what you want, or think, they will.

It requires the marketing round be completely integrated, or people won't be able to find it. If PR and marketing are creating content, but the community manager, social media team, or sales team isn't involved, it won't go anywhere quickly.

User-Generated Content

One of the biggest challenges for most companies is content. It's hard to produce, it's difficult to engage customers and prospects, and those producing the content aren't typically the technical professionals. So they turn to user-generated content. But there are other risks in opening up the company to allow customers to create content.

While the resources needed aren't as great as if you're producing your own content, you still need someone for oversight and moderation.

Take, for instance, the 12 Most blog. When founders Sean McGinnis and Dan Newman opened it to their community, they discovered users were submitting content for publication they had stolen from other sites.

It's imperative you do a quick Google search to be sure the content you're receiving hasn't been used anywhere else.

Until you actually begin to use user-generated content, you won't be able to finalize policies, structure, and use. It needs to be fluid, flexible, and nimble, which can be a challenge if the legal department has to be involved in all approvals.

Crowdsourcing

In 2010, Gap used crowdsourcing to create a new logo as part of the 1969 clothing line brand launch. It held a contest among designers, and the person who created the winning logo would get public awareness of its design through the launch by Gap and a feature in the 99designs (the company that managed the contest) newsletter. It launched its new logo and got myriad complaints from the very vocal blogosphere. Complaints varied from "it's ugly" to "it doesn't support the Gap brand." Gap caved to pressure and changed its logo back to the one it has used for more than 20 years.

Supporting customers is a burden, and it's time-intensive. If you ask for their opinions, you have to be sure to listen and incorporate their feedback. If any tactic needs ego stroking, it is crowdsourcing. If you do not listen or act upon the feedback, it's worse than not asking at all. Be prepared to make significant changes if you go down this road.

It might end up that a very vocal minority does not like what you're doing through crowdsourcing and won't be shy about telling you so. Before you open yourself up, make sure the thick skin is grown and you understand the strategy behind why you're doing it. You'll repeat it over and over again.

Social Media

Social media has become the shiny new penny everyone thinks they must use. Too often, though, you see companies building a Facebook page, getting on Twitter, or using Google+ without a strategy, without understanding how it works, and without tying their efforts to a real return on investment.

Not all of your customers use social media, either personally or professionally—so the idea that you will reach them all on one of the platforms is not valid. If you're using brand monitoring and listening, you'll quickly learn which social tools your audiences are using. Don't create a free-for-all and build platforms on every network. Really understand who you're trying to target and where they spend time online.

Even though it's free to create pages and profiles, social media is not free in terms of time and effort. It can be quite costly if done correctly. And, to that point, the return on investment is delayed. You are building relationships with human beings, and that takes time. Also, some of the relationships you build through social media will never turn into customers, so you have to manage who becomes a customer, a brand ambassador, a member of your referral network, or just a taker.

The tools change frighteningly quickly. Rather than becoming really good at using the tools, the marketing round should be really good at driving business using the tools that are available.

Exercises

Monitoring Program

If the marketing round doesn't already have a monitoring program in place, that is the first step to your groundswell approach. There are many ways you can begin, using free tools that will give you enough information to make informed decisions.

The tools are as follows:

- Google Alerts remains the most effective free way to monitor the conversations. Because it monitors the entire Web—Web sites, blogs, social networks, comments, and more—and delivers everything to you in one daily email, it's the best overall tool.

- Twitter search (search.twitter.com) is a free way to monitor what is (or is not) being said on Twitter.

- Using a Twitter desktop application (TweetDeck, HootSuite, MarketMeSuite, and so on) allows you to create searches on any of the social networks and have a column that brings results directly to you, when you have the app open. Some of the apps are free, whereas others charge for certain types of results.

After you've decided which tools you're going to use, work in the marketing round to determine which searches you want to include:

- The company name
- The product or services name(s)
- The industry
- Key competitors
- Executive names
- Companies you admire
- Key people who work for competitors
- The company name plus the word "sucks"
- Typical misspellings of the company or brand names
- Any type of negative feedback you've heard

At some point, you'll need to graduate from the free monitoring tools to paid ones. You'll know when you get to that point because the alerts will become overwhelming. That could be 200 or 10,000 mentions. When you get to that point, consider tools such as Radian6 (inside Salesforce), Sysomos, or Spiral16.

Determine Groundswell Tactics

In Chapter 2, "Know All the Tools," you worked through the marketing round assets and learned in which phase (crawl, walk, run, fly) you would use each. In Table 7.1 you'll do the same, except with the groundswell tactics.

Table 7.1   Determine the Usefulness of Groundswell Tactics

Tactic	Going to Use?	Crawl, Walk, Run, or Fly Phase	Responsible
EXAMPLE: Owned content	Yes	Crawl	Public relations, corporate communication
Brand Monitoring			
Word of Mouth			
Brand Ambassadors			
Public Communities			
Private Communities			
Owned Content			
User-Generated Content			
Crowdsourcing			
Social Media			

Endnotes

1. http://womma.org/wom101/.

2. www.roiresearch.com/blog/.

3. www.thelaughingcow.com/blog.

8

When to Deploy Flanking Techniques

The approaches discussed so far—the middle, top, and bottom—are all from the social, public relations, networking, or direct marketing disciplines. Each takes the tactical knowledge from those disciplines and approaches the customer from a unique standpoint to afford an advantage.

But sometimes your marketing round has no community in place at all, little opportunity to engage with the media and influencers, and no time or means to use a direct approach. That is when you use communications disciplines to flank your customers, approaching them in unexpected ways.

Flanking is the traditional military approach of going around an enemy's side, either the right or the left, to attack in an unexpected fashion. When successful, the flanking army often finds itself with a successful two-front approach that yields victory on the battlefield. Customers are not enemies, but their resistance to traditional marketing can be so strong that a "flanking" technique needs to be deployed to simply get their attention.

There are a wide variety of reasons to use flanking techniques: Your company may not have any market attention as a start-up. You may have a new product or an old established one, and the media doesn't find your story newsworthy. You may be up against an entrenched market leader.

Perhaps there are market factors, such as legal constraints that bar communications. Or maybe there is a public issue—a failure or a crisis—that has tarnished your reputation.

In such cases, advertising, guerrilla marketing, or press blitzes and events could become primary thrusts for your communications effort.

Many businesses use such flanking techniques—not every company has a terrific news peg, the luxury of direct marketing, or a huge social media community. Even established brands often engage in flanking to reach new customers because they have exhausted the news value of their products, because customers have not opted in to their direct marketing lists, or because stakeholders have no interest in participating in corporate social media.

So don't see this technique as a corner from which to escape. It simply is the reality of your marketplace. This is particularly true of business-to-business marketing rounds. Flanking techniques may be your only path for reaching your customer.

Washington, D.C., is home to the nation's biggest customer for a wide variety of products, including armaments, IT, and products like toilet paper. According to the Department of Defense (DoD), it will have a base budget of $518 billion before special expenditures to fund the operations in Afghanistan and Iraq. Those wars add another $115 billion to the DoD's 2012 fiscal year operations.[1]

But you won't find defense contractors Lockheed Martin, Northrop Grumman, Boeing, and General Dynamics generating major coverage from the local news media. Nor will you see these companies doing much more with social media than recruiting employees. Discussing "collateral damage," military-speak for civilian deaths in the process of war, on Facebook isn't popular.

Nor can they rely on direct mail to reach the DoD, thanks to the anthrax crisis of 2001. They can't rely on branded knickknacks and other gifts, because the federal gift rule limits what employees can accept.[2] Even email is pretty much an opt-in game.

So, what's left? Highly targeted flanking techniques.

These contractors buy advertising sponsorships and pitch placements in such trade media products as Federal News Radio, *Army Times,* and *Federal Computer Week.* They buy advertising space at the Pentagon Metro station and surrounding bus stops. General Dynamics sponsors special seats for veterans at Washington Capitals hockey games.

To get a leg up in the PR market, they hire firms that already have coveted relationships with editors of defense-industry publications. And to meet customers face to face, defense contractors pony up big bucks to attend conferences and networking events.

Sometimes they still can't get access. So they hire retiring generals and admirals to get access to their Rolodexes.

Consider how many millions of dollars these vendors are spending to get in front of relatively small groups of buyers; only 5, 10, maybe 20 people touch multimillion-dollar contract approvals. But in the defense industry, vendors have no other choice.

That makes marketing to the DoD a prime example of the use of multiple flanking techniques. Most industries don't require that companies go to such lengths, but for a one-stop primer on ways to reach your customers, the DoD is great.

Here are the forms of communications that most marketing rounds use to flank:

- Advertising
- Guerrilla marketing
- Event marketing and networking
- Trickle-up media relations

Guerrilla marketing is the most creative and surprising of the tactics. Its wide-ranging definition can encompass high-cost staged events and simple flash mobs. More often than not, a guerrilla tactic involves an Internet stunt like Blendtec's videos of its machines shredding things, or a live event, like Heineken's staging of a fake broadcast arts event at a theater during a Milan AC/Real Madrid game in Italy in October 2009.

When considering guerrilla tactics, the marketing round often deals with the dreaded request for "viral video." The odds of your organization's actually publishing a YouTube video and its going viral without significant help from a marketing agency or a massive social media following are akin to the odds of your winning the lottery jackpot.

You should remember that the definition of "viral" is relative. Most videos are watched only a few times—one that nets thousands of views is well above YouTube's average, and tens of thousands is successful by almost every barometer—except in the world of viral videos, where if you don't reach at least 50,000 views, you haven't made it.

To go viral, many companies resort to gimmicks. Air New Zealand achieved its first viral video success in 2009, but at the expense of the dignity of its employees—its CEO and other male and female staff members appeared wearing only body paint.

Nike's 2007 "Run on Air" campaign during International Car Free Day in Prague is an example of a relatively low-cost guerrilla marketing success. The company placed hundreds of cardboard "boots" featuring Nike Air shoes on the front tires of many cars, with "parking tickets" that said Run on Air. The campaign turned heads throughout Prague and got international media attention. Further, video footage of Czechs reacting to the cardboard boots was released on YouTube. Its minor viral success triggered further coverage in the blogosphere, including by social media mainstay Mashable.

The total cost of the Nike campaign, which generated fantastic publicity, was relatively small: creative development costs for the cardboard boots and tickets, then paying someone to drive around Prague and place the ads. The campaign was more cost-effective than a major media initiative.

Flanking really gets down to putting yourself in front of customers when they don't expect to see you. Whether that occurs in a traditional place like a magazine or in a crazy guerrilla campaign depends on your company's culture, creativity, and opportunities to get in front of customers.

Benefits of Flanking Approaches

The primary purpose of a flanking approach is to build goodwill with customers when using all other means is difficult or unlikely. Second, you're putting yourself in front of customers when you know they will be in a certain place. Many flanking techniques are expensive, but they may offer intangible benefits that other marketing approaches don't. Here's a look at some of the benefits of flanking approaches.

Advertising

Advertising is the most common flanking technique, allowing companies to pay for specific placement in a wide variety of media. In the U.S., advertisers spent $131 billion to get the word out about their products and services.[3] Here are the primary benefits of advertising:

- You can reach customers anytime, anywhere through ad spends.
- You have diverse choices: Whether it's the use of transportation, radio, search, and billboard advertising to reach commuting consumers, or buying placement on niche Web sites and trade magazines to touch B2B buyers, your company can find customers.
- Advertising allows your company to completely control the message in purchased media.
- Your marketing round can push its brand and generate sales. Branding can build and protect reputation when the media won't, while lead generation and sales directly affect the bottom line.
- Calls to action, including custom URLs, allow you to determine how successful your ads are.
- Calls to action allow you to cultivate interested customers who self-identify with email or mailing addresses, which gives you a ready-made list for direct marketing pitches.
- Advertising conveys a level of legitimacy. If your company can afford to advertise, it often is perceived as stable.
- Successful word-of-mouth marketing is typically supported with an advertising campaign, which sustains and fuels buzz.

Guerrilla Marketing

This is the lowest-cost group of tactics within the flanking techniques. It is also the most wide-ranging. Here are the benefits of guerrilla tactics:

- Guerrilla marketing allows for free-form creativity in ways that other media cannot. The sky is the limit.

- Aggressive tactics are welcome. Standing out is necessary for your effort to succeed.

- These types of tactics are relatively low-cost to produce, particularly if they are Internet-centric.

- You can create a mini campaign that rides the coattails of another event, whether it is a holiday or a trade show or convention.

- If you choose to target a physical event, you have a captive audience that will be in place for whatever marketing activity you plan.

- If successful, these tactics tend to create a ton of buzz, and they give your brand an opportunity to stand out as fresh and exciting.

Event Marketing and Networking

There's nothing quite like feet on the street. In essence, that is what event marketing accomplishes for your organization. When you are an unknown brand without predeveloped relationships, event marketing becomes a flanking technique. It can be cost-effective if you simply send business developers to "work the room." And the benefits can only increase with your marketing round's investment. Here are some of the benefits of event marketing and networking:

- Events can do more than direct-market to stakeholders, which may be ineffective if they don't know who you are. You can brand and create buzz for your brand.

- Your marketing round can target events that are most likely to attract customers. Usually, lists of customers or companies attending are available in advance.

- Paid opportunities are available at most events, allowing access beyond simple attendance.

- A well-attended event populated by customers, media, and bloggers can be used to stage major marketing initiatives, including trade booths, guerrilla marketing initiatives, strategic sponsorships, and media programs.

- Speaking opportunities can be pitched in advance of an event.

Trickle-Up Media Relations

Not every company can afford the cost of advertising. That's why many turn to the media and bloggers. (This is the top-down approach discussed in Chapter 6.) But there are fewer and fewer mainstream media outlets that report on business stories. Even local business journals are inundated with publicity requests. So companies have to work their way into the media and customers' minds through "trickle-up" media relations.

Getting a big break with a story rarely happens anymore without a savvy PR firm that can help develop pitches. Further, many companies have to earn their credibility one publication at a time before a national or major metropolitan media outlet will consider them. Here are some examples of how smaller media publications and trade-related blogs can help:

- Credibility builds with each media hit; your company message becomes increasingly viable with each masthead that writes about it.

- Customers are more likely to trust a story than they are to trust an advertisement.

- Though trade press and topic-specific blogs have smaller readerships, they are considered more authoritative than mainstream media by some stakeholders because that readership has a high level of expertise.

- Niche media reporters and bloggers are often quoted by mainstream media outlets as subject-matter experts. Informing them can provide an indirect route into the mainstream press.

- Larger media outlets and blogs read smaller outlets to get story ideas. A smaller-market story can break it open for your marketing round, cascading into many more outlets.

Risks of Flanking Approaches

Taking a flanking approach has more risk than other tactics; flanking almost always involves an unexpected touch with your potential customer. In the worst cases, that contact is unwanted.

This demands high-quality marketing to make your effort stand out from the other messages people receive on a daily basis from friends, news organizations, and media, as well as every other company and organization pushing its own message. The following are weaknesses in the four types of flanking approaches.

Advertising

The most obvious risk of advertising is its high cost. But there are other risks involved:

- Extremely high costs exist for both placement and creative, the latter of which often is overlooked when the marketing budget is being set. But without strong creative work, advertising is less likely to succeed.

- Substandard creative work can sink advertising into mediocre marketing, or worse, spark customer outrage.

- Finding the best advertising opportunities requires a research investment for your marketing round. Which media are most likely to produce the desired results?

- ROI is significantly lower than with direct marketing, with estimates as low as $4 returned for every dollar spent, according to the Direct Marketing Association.

- Customers are skeptical of advertising messages and don't readily accept them as fact.

Guerrilla Marketing

Taking this tack can be the most fun, but it also has the highest risk of failure. Because success relies on creativity and the ability to stand out, most corporate marketers are not willing to take the risks necessary to succeed with guerrilla tactics.

Consider Network Solutions' "Go Granny" viral video success starring Cloris Leachman, who played a foul-mouthed, over-the-hill model taking Go Daddy girls to task for Go Daddy's demeaning advertising approach towards women. Not many companies have the moxie to release a YouTube video like that.

Other risks of guerrilla marketing include these:

- It demands significant out-of-the box creativity and this may require your company to seek expensive outside help.

- In the quest for the viral video, a company invests significant amounts of repeated energy into bad content creation that yields little results. Time is money.

- Some guerrilla attempts can be perceived as extremely offensive, tarnishing a brand. For example, Kenneth Cole got in hot water for claiming that the Arab Spring protests in Egypt were occurring because of its hot 2011 spring line of shoes.

- A viral marketing attempt may land your marketing round in trouble with the authorities. Public events, flash mobs, and so on can occur with or without the sanction of the event organizer, a private property owner, or the law. When they happen without, legal issues can arise.

Event Marketing and Networking

Event marketing has its negatives, beginning with questionable return on investment. Unlike advertising, which at least has some guarantee that your marketing will be viewed, event marketing depends completely on your team's strengths, from targeting the right event to branding and your ability to create buzz.

Here are some things to be wary of when considering an event:

- Without access to key customers, you cannot guarantee even an opportunity for success.
- Scheduling meetings in advance requires significant work leading up to an event, from development to direct marketing efforts.
- Costs can be high. At a high-dollar B2B trade show, a deal has to close for the investment to be worthwhile.
- With business-to-business events, the length of time between the event and any resulting sale can stretch into months or even a year.

Trickle-Up Media Relations

The risk with trickle-up media relations is that you can invest a lot time and never get coverage. And if you do get coverage, the financial results are highly subjective. You may get a phone call or a surge of Web traffic, but generally speaking, the primary benefits are brand credibility, more media mentions, and opportunities such as email sign-ups. Companies looking for direct financial benefit won't be immediately happy. Here are some other risks:

- Most reputable media relations firms will charge your company at least $10,000 per month. National firms cost even more.
- Even with professional help, your story may not be newsworthy.
- Once you speak with the media or a blogger, you have no control over the message. If you don't like what is said, getting a retraction or correction could cost you the relationship with the media outlet. Plus, it will likely be in small print on an inside page of the publication.
- The smaller the media outlet, the more likely your company may be asked to "pay to play." This means that, without advertising or exhibiting with the media company, they will not write about your company.
- Some media outlets are so short on reporters that your only opportunity may be to write an article yourself and submit it

through the publication's online submission process. This creates
a time demand for your marketing round.

Determining Your Flanking Approach

So what's the best path to take? The answer: It depends—on your budget,
and on your strengths, and on the results of your market research.

Flanking can be fun, particularly with guerrilla tactics. It empowers experimentation and innovation, and who wouldn't want to launch a big, buzz-
worthy marketing hit? But you may not have the luxury of that choice.

How tolerant is your company of culture shock? Will your culture allow
you to do something against the grain? Going back to the defense-
contractor example, Lockheed Martin probably won't sanction the production of a campy, humorous video.

Can your company afford to advertise? And not just once? You need to
advertise with enough frequency to drive your message home to your stakeholders.

That said, there are many low-cost opportunities to advertise. There are
search engine–based and online advertising programs. Radio and public
transportation–based advertising are powerful ways to reach a metropolitan
marketplace. Cable TV can offer low-cost access. Social ads on Facebook
and other media can be great low-cost ways to brand your company.

Regardless of the medium, you need to support your advertising buy. That
includes the cost of placement and the cost of creating the campaign to
begin with.

Events and trickle-up media relations are more conservative and cost-
effective, but they are less likely to produce runaway successes. They are
"blue-chip" flanking techniques that offer fundamental marketing opportunities, but they require your marketing round to have the skills and savvy
to produce results.

Most important, the goal of flanking is to build a loyal customer base.
Incorporate calls to action so your marketing round can use your effort to
gather contact information for later direct marketing, media relationship,
and online community development.

Exercises

Media Planning

Companies that engage in advertising regularly hire firms to develop their campaigns and to suggest which media to buy into. But many companies choose to source their own media buys for a couple of reasons:

1. Advertising agencies often receive a 10 percent or higher cut of the media placement fees.

2. Good agencies recommend the media they think is best for the client. But they may not show you all the properties on the table. And lesser-quality agencies have been known to play favorites with media representatives. This can create issues for a company that wants a full picture.

Exploring your own media buy can be a great way to find out if your marketing round is serious about advertising. To execute a cursory sampling of media purchases, take the following steps:

1. Write down your budget for media purchases.

2. List media that your stakeholders commonly use. Include trade media, national media, local media, and broadcast and Internet properties.

3. Find the publisher or advertising representative's phone number for each media outlet, call, and ask for their media kit or rates (be prepared for some hustling on the phone).

4. Take your calendar of marketing and industry events, and copy it over to an Excel sheet.

5. Add a line to the Excel sheet for each media property.

6. Plan to spend advertising dollars for the select media against each of the events.

7. Total up the costs for each of the buys.

From here, you can see how much the advertising spend would be for the media. Keep in mind you have yet to negotiate with the media outlets, and often you can get costs as high as 30 percent or more depending on frequency and length of commitment. Remember, however, that you have yet to pay for any creative work (unless you have your own creative department).

Usually at this point, you'll need to eliminate a few of the media outlets, and perhaps reduce frequency to make it doable. Or you may have sticker shock and realize that advertising is not the right course for your marketing round.

Endnotes

1. Roxana Tiron, *Bloomberg Business News,* December 15, 2011, http://mobile.bloomberg.com/news/2011-12-15/u-s-congress-approves-662-billion-defense-plan-headed-to-obama.

2. U.S. Department of Justice, "Do It Right," www.justice.gov/jmd/ethics/generalf.htm#3.

3. www.hollywoodreporter.com/news/us-advertising-spending-rose-65-168793.

9

Integration

Now that you understand the different media types and the different techniques, it's time to put them all together. You're going to face different levels of integration: horizontal, vertical, internal, external, and data. What you want, however, is a complete circle that fluidly incorporates all the levels into one. Hence, the marketing round.

To better understand how you're going to integrate, look at each of the levels.

Horizontal Integration

Horizontal integration is across business functions, such as finance, sales, distribution, marketing, and communication. All the business functions work together and are conscious of how their decisions and actions affect customers. It occurs when the entire company is working toward one vision and one goal without the handicap of silos.

FedEx has marketing activities centered on customer segments. A cross-functional team staffs each audience with a manager, a marketer, an analyst, someone from fulfillment, and at least one person from the advertising and PR agencies.

This is a great example of horizontal integration, but because it's broken down by each customer segment and doesn't have an overall company team, it hasn't yet reached the marketing round.

Vertical Integration

Vertical integration means marketing objectives support the higher-level corporate goals, strategies, and vision. The marketing round has a vertical integration foundation because everything you do is going to support the company's vision and goals, resulting in increased sales and profits.

Internal Integration

Internal integration, typically known as corporate communication, keeps all employees informed and motivated about new developments, from new ads or branding to new services or strategic partners. Many companies don't have a focus on employees. This must change in the marketing round.

External Integration

External integration requires external partners to work closely together to deliver one solution. For companies, this means your advertising, marketing, and public relations firms are all working well together in one sandbox. For agencies, this means you're partnering with other professionals or firms to better suit the needs of your clients.

Data Integration

It won't come as a surprise to you that data isn't shared across company business functions. Simple things such as Google analytics or margin percentages are hard to come by in most companies. In data integration, information is shared among all internal audiences in order to best serve the company.

Marketing in the Round

The marketing round becomes an integration of everything: horizontal, vertical, internal, external, and data. It becomes a complete round of information, knowledge, and wisdom in order to achieve company goals and work toward the vision. As discussed in previous chapters, it's important that your executive team support this mission because you won't be able to completely integrate without it.

Mapping to Resources

You may have a large marketing team or you may be working alone, but one thing is certain: Your needs won't be the same as those of any other reader of this book. It's important to map the specific resources you have available, not to wish you had more or imagine what you could do with more.

Something that works for any size company and any size marketing team is starting with a zero budget. It allows you to start from scratch, building your plan based on the idea that you have no money to spend. All you have is the time and talents of the people in your marketing round.

Using the company's stated goals and vision, determine what the marketing round's objectives are for moving the business forward. Consider everything you can do in a full year—without a budget.

Then you can add in your budget and prioritize your goals, based on how much they'll cost to execute. In some cases the budget will be people's time (groundswell), and in others it will be hard costs (top down).

All of this should be done in the first four meetings of the marketing round. Your meetings should occur at least weekly until you begin to execute. During your marketing round meetings, integration should be a topic of discussion. It also should be included in the full company staff meetings. The more you talk about integration and what it means, the more likely it is to happen.

But it's also important that integration includes customers. Your marketing round should be wrapped around customers' buying processes, where they find you, how they engage with you, and how to anticipate their future needs. Select the techniques, approaches, and tactics that are right for your customers, and develop activities that keep them coming—and coming back—to you.

To do this, the marketing round should be working with sales and customer service to develop strong relationships with customers. Ask customers for feedback and really listen to what they have to say. Then incorporate their feedback into your strategies and methods to better integrate them into your system of communication.

And you should be prepared to change. The only consistent thing in today's digital world is change, so don't be averse to it. Your marketing-round plan may work really well for 90 days, and then customers may react negatively to something. You'll have to be flexible enough to react in a positive way that keeps customers happy and moves the company closer to its vision. Some things will always work really well, while others may work for only a short time. Don't give in to the "shiny object" syndrome; don't ditch an effective tool just to try something new.

Determining Approaches and Tactics

At first, it's going to be fairly easy to determine which approaches and tactics you use. Look at the strengths of the people in your marketing round. Some may be really strong in search and email marketing, while others excel at writing and communication. The methods your team is strong in should be at the top of your must-do list.

Then, working with sales, customer service, product development, your executive team, and anyone else who touches a customer, discuss how those customers find you.

They may find you through trade shows, conferences, cold-calling, articles in print publications, and advertising. You don't want to stop doing the things that generate leads right now. But you're going to add approaches and tactics that generate leads for the future.

If your team is strong on writing and search, you'll want to add inbound marketing and search engine optimization. Perhaps you can stretch a bit and add search engine marketing and social media. But remember, in Chapter 7, "The Groundswell Approach," you determined which social tools are important for you to use. So don't go all gangbusters on Twitter if your audience isn't there. Use the monitoring taught in that chapter to learn which social tools make sense for your current and future customers.

Once you decide which approaches work right now and which ones you're going to try out, you want to test, test, and test some more.

Following are some examples of things you can test and how to get the data you need to make informed decisions.

Email Marketing

Email marketing tends to be the forgotten stepchild, but it's still extremely effective. Everyone uses email. We may not love it; we may consider it a necessary evil. But we all use it. How you rise above the level of spam will depend on how you test and what kind of value you provide to your recipients.

It's important to determine when you have the most click-throughs (not opens) by sending on different days and different times to see when your audiences are most engaged with your content. For some it may be Saturdays at 8 a.m. and for others it may be Wednesdays at 7 p.m. You won't know what works best for you until you test it.

Also test different types of content and calls to action, based on who is reading what, who is sharing, and how many people are clicking through and doing something you would like them to do. Variables like subject lines, layout, and design may affect engagement. Test them, too.

Content Marketing

Your content marketing could be anything, from a blog or white paper campaign to videos or podcasts. Blogging is, by far, the most effective content (or inbound) marketing, but it also is the most time-intensive. If you don't have the resources or expertise for blogging, bite off a smaller chunk with other types of content.

You should test headlines, calls to action, content, traffic generators (search, social media, advertising), and different products or services.

When you're testing your headlines, you may find that lists (top ten ways to do something) or numbers (five marketing ideas that drive results) do better than something controversial. Or you may find the exact opposite. If you test, test, and test some more, and then measure and refine, you'll find what works for you, not necessarily what works for the pundit in your industry.

One of the biggest mistakes most marketers make in content marketing is they forget about the call to action. Because content marketing is seen as valuable and educational, it seems counterproductive to sell. But there are ways to create your calls to action so that they're not seen as selling.

For instance, provide a coupon or discount on a featured product of the week. Or provide downloads of white papers or eBooks that give more information that is valuable and educational. Whatever you do, test the effectiveness of each approach.

Search Engine Optimization

Google continues to change its algorithms, so it's nearly a full-time job to stay up-to-date on what is new and what you need to change on your Web properties in order to be found in searches. At the time of this writing, Google significantly changed search with Google Plus Your World. Personal search results now appear at the top of the page. This is great for the products or services your family, friends, brand ambassadors, and loyalists recommend. But it also is rumored they soon will return direct searches, which means a person won't have to go to your site to get the information they need. Rather, Google will give it directly to them on the search page.

Subscribe to SEOmoz, TopRank, ClickZ, or Google News Inside to keep the marketing round educated on changes. TopRank[1] does a ranking every year of all the search-related blogs (warning: there are a lot), if you want to check out some others.

And...test.

You'll want to test keywords, content, and geotargeting.

The easiest first step to testing your keywords is to Google them. How many pages come up for what you'd like to use? Do your competitors show up on the first page? This will begin to educate you on how much work you have ahead of you.

Then, in tandem with your content marketing, you're going to test those keywords in different pieces of content. What is ranking you higher? What isn't ranking you at all? This will begin to tell you what and how people are searching in order to find you.

And, if you're a local business, you want to test the performance of different keywords that include your location. For instance, think about combinations such as Italian food in Raleigh or dentists in Fargo or oxidizers in Dallas. Whatever it happens to be, you want to test your keywords with the geography.

Search Engine Marketing

Search engine marketing (SEM) isn't used very often, but it's extremely effective. Typically known as pay-per-click or Google AdWords, SEM combines that with some very targeted keywords and landing pages that have specific calls to action.

You want to test keyword variations, messaging, landing pages, calls to action, ads, required information, and even the layout and design of the landing pages and ads.

If this is all new to you, read *Always Be Testing*, by Bryan Eisenberg. It will help you understand SEM, its effectiveness, and how to test your work.

The most important things to SEM are the keywords, the landing pages, and the messaging in the ads. These three things you'll want to test separately and together.

As you choose your tactics, you should summarize what they are, why you are going to use them, what results you expect, how you'll test them, and the budget. If the results you expect aren't going to be tied to a specific dollar amount (brand awareness, credibility, thought leadership), be sure you describe how that will dovetail with a tactic that is tied to a monetary return.

Tips for a Unified Brand

In January of 2010, Conan O'Brien lost his job as host of *The Tonight Show* in front of the entire world. As Lisa Barone wrote in her blog, Outspoken Media,[2] he "handled it like a professional. With the help of the Internet, he was able to brand himself as the people's hero. Team Conan was created to honor the quirky giant, and he bid farewell to NBC in style, eventually embarking on a cross-country comedy tour—a tour that was possible, in part, because of the positive buzz and following created through Team Conan.

"In January, the Conan brand was full of energy, life and a spirit of screwing 'the man.' It was something everyone could identify with. And it stayed that way for months.

"It stayed that way until May of that same year when he sat down to talk to *60 Minutes.*"

That interview torpedoed "the perception and conversation around the Conan brand. Instead of seeing Conan as a humble and charismatic man who once spoke to the 'people of Earth,' he resurfaced bearded and beaten. He seemed increasingly bitter over what happened, taking serious (and awkward) jabs at NBC and [Jay] Leno, and halfheartedly telling us not to feel sorry for him when it was clear he was feeling sorry for himself. He lost the grace he had in January, appearing more like a jilted bride who, three months after the would-be wedding date, still falls asleep in her wedding dress crying and cursing the man that put her there."

Creating a unified brand isn't easy, especially when you're combining your offline brand with your online brand. But, as was the case with Conan, if the brand isn't presented consistently, in all venues, it's confusing and unsettling.

The job of the marketing round is to determine not just the brand image, but also the brand message, and stick with it. Are you hip and trendy, like Apple? Do you do no evil, like Google? Or do you want to stick it to the man, like Conan?

Think about those three examples. Apple, while maintaining its hip and trendy brand message, also isn't open platform, which makes the tech community opposed to its products.

Google, in some people's eyes, does lots of evil and hasn't been able to maintain its brand message as it ventures out of its search-industry niche.

Conan was shouting "screw the man" messages online and in print interviews, but he wasn't able to present that image when interviewed in person.

Your brand is about the entire experience for your customers. Get to know them. Go on sales calls. Listen in on customer calls. Interact with them online. That way you can work with your sales and customer service teams to build a consistent brand message, and you can back it up when those customers engage your business or cause "in real life."

Consider people you get to know through social networks; maybe you talk to them every day on Twitter. You develop a perception of them. Is it unsettling when you meet them in person, and their reality doesn't match that perception? Like radio personalities who don't "look like they sound"?

This can happen to your brand. For Conan, the brand is him. For your company, the brand is what customers perceive it to be. If what you say the brand is doesn't match how customers perceive it, you're not delivering the promise. It's your job to enhance, build, and portray a brand that matches the customer's perception.

Exercises

Mapping Resources

This exercise allows you to take a hard look at the people within your marketing round and determine their strengths and their expertise. It also allows you to figure out where you have holes so you know which resources you'll eventually need to add.

Table 9.1   Mapping Resources

Person	Strengths	Expertise
EXAMPLE: Team member #1	Corporate communication, content development, engagement	Public relations, search

Determine Approaches and Tactics

Although this chapter doesn't explore every tactic the marketing round can use, it gives you a good starting point. This exercise will help you determine which approaches to use and how to test and refine the tactics you choose.

Table 9.2 Determine Approaches and Tactics

Tactic	Tests	Results
EXAMPLE: Email marketing	Times of day sent, days of week sent, subject lines, content, calls to action, click-throughs	Tuesdays at 8 a.m. have 20 percent more click-throughs

Create a Unified Brand

Only you can determine the brand and how customers perceive it in the marketplace. The best way to do this is to go on sales calls, listen in on customer service calls, monitor the Twitter stream, or engage with customers in other online communities. Really listen to what is being said and be prepared to make changes to your messaging, your tactics, your approaches, and your strategies based on what you're hearing.

Endnotes

1. TopRank listing of search-related blogs, www.toprankblog.com/search-marketing-blogs/.

2. http://outspokenmedia.com/reputation-management/are-you-creating-a-unified-brand/.

10

Plan the Entire Tactical Effort

Many strategic plans end at the selection of tactics. From there, most practitioners take their marching orders back to their desks and create plans specific to their silos.

This is not enough. You must envision the entire program across all channels, plan it out in an efficient manner, and time the delivery of your efforts appropriately.

Consider this:

- *If timed to work together, your media relations effort can provide credibility and air cover for your direct marketing, bolstering your conversion rate.*
- *Social media conversations and blog posts can help journalists find your story credible and your product worth buying.*
- *Strategic advertising in a campaign can heighten the buzz-worthiness of your online social effort.*
- *Local, national, or industry events, a specific holiday, or a manufactured event creates a captive audience, again fostering buzz.*

Whether it's a methodical daily commitment to communicate with a community, or a sudden burst of activity to market a new product or launch an advocacy campaign, your marketing round's actions must be planned. Together, your marketing efforts are substantively stronger.

Consider the whole purpose of multichannel or integrated marketing—it acknowledges the very real nature of human behavior and media use.

No one goes home and "Facebooks" for three solid hours. Nor is their primary source of information radio advertisements on the local rock station. Instead people tend to read, watch, and listen to multiple forms of media throughout the day, and even at the same time.

People are bombarded by messages, stories, and information at an unprecedented level. Public restrooms are now fair game for advertising messages. These messages converge from many sources to provide a unique experience. In turn, people are becoming accustomed to multichannel experiences as a normal media pattern.

Consider the phenomenon of social TV, in which people watch broadcast or cable TV programming while updating their social networks on their phones, tablets, or laptops. A whole new type of programming is arising to meet the social TV trend.

Your own experiences probably confirm the growing reality of confluent information streams: It's hard to remember where you first heard about many products and services.

Successful campaigns take advantage of this phenomenon with a little bit of everything. Consider Greater Washington's Give to the Max Day: A consumer campaign marketed by online start-up Razoo raised $2 million from 18,000 donors for local nonprofits in one day. Its success was rooted in its staged consumer marketing—starting with subway and bus advertising three weeks before the event, then radio advertisements, then select TV advertisements, and then an incredible flurry of media relations the week preceding the event. All along, the entire effort was supported by social media and blogger relations.

Master Your Calendar

The first step in building your tactical plan is understanding the marketing round's calendar of events. Each group has different events, launches, and initiatives throughout the year.

It is likely that your industry has its own events. For example, the Consumer Electronics Show happens every January, when the tech industry highlights its products, real and in development, for the coming year. Your competitors may already have scheduled public events. And then there are your country's holidays and seasonal vacations to consider. These holidays naturally dictate marketing. B2B marketers are likely to avoid the winter holiday season, while consumer marketers will build their entire fourth quarter effort on the weeks between Thanksgiving and Christmas.

Take all of these events and put them on a universal calendar. Color-code it so that each group is represented and identified (see Figure 10.1), and then make it accessible so that each marketing-round member can add events.

Now it is time to analyze that calendar. Identify several key factors for your campaign:

- How early in the year (or quarter) do you need to act to meet your marketing goals?
- If you launch at an industry event, will you be able to rise above the noise?
- Are there open periods of time that lend themselves to a launch or general communications?
- Does the potential timing provide any conflicts internally or externally? Can the program overcome them or are they insurmountable barriers?
- Do you have the resources to make the effort happen in the optimal time frame?

Sample Calendar

Activity	October					November				December			
	1	8	15	22	29	5	12	19	26	3	10	17	24
Federal Holidays		X				X	X						X
Industry Events						RetailTech							
Advertising		C.Day								Holiday Campaigns			
Direct Marketing		C.Day								Holiday Campaigns			
PR				3Q Financial						Holiday Campaigns			
Interactive/Social								Vet D	Thanksgiving				Xmas

Figure 10.1 *Color-coded sample calendar.*

The calendar is a great tool because it helps your marketing round identify opportunities when stakeholders and your organization can best communicate. It provides context and framing to a marketing initiative.

Understanding the Resources at Play

So you know which tactics you want to use, but are they available? Does your marketing round—and specifically the tactical practitioners who are leading your marketing effort—have the resources necessary to succeed?

Is there enough human resource capacity to wage a marketing program? If not, are there enough monetary resources to hire a staffer, a consultant, or an agency (or extend the current scope of work with your preferred agency)?

Consider creative and media costs. If advertising will be used—even in just a supporting role—can you pay for a creative campaign? Or just an ad? Does the marketing round have any prepurchased media inventory? If not, can you afford it?

What about interactive? Do you have or need to purchase development resources? Is an online expenditure needed? Do you have the resources to have people present and to create content for social media tactics?

From a media relations standpoint, is there an obvious story? Does an event need to be planned to create news? Or will speaking at another event achieve our objective?

Does the event team (or budget, if a single person handles multiple roles) need to sponsor an event? Do they need to be present? Is there travel budget for the event?

What about sales, customer service, legal, and other members of the round-table? Do they need to be involved and prepped for the effort? Will it require expenditures on their part?

As you can see, there are many, many resource questions that come into play. Be sure you have the full picture so that managing your marketing effort becomes a question of execution rather than an internal battle for resources throughout the life of the campaign.

Timing: Which Tactics Should Lead?

Timing and sequencing is an essential part of classic strategy. Consider what our sage Musashi says about it in *The Book of Five Rings*:

"There is timing in everything.... From the outset you must know the applicable timing and the inapplicable timing, and from among the large and small things and the fast and slow timings find the relevant timing, first seeing the distance timing and the background timing. This is the main thing in strategy."

When you a have a lead tactic, when you know when to act and with which resources, it is time to start planning. By now you almost certainly know what the centerpieces of your marketing campaign will be.

That doesn't mean you should run out the door and start. But many people want to flip a switch on their campaign. You can almost hear them say, "This is the launch date—let's go!" In a competitive environment, that can be a mistake that brings lesser results.

In particular, without the full support of your marketing round, it is unlikely your message will resonate. Customers are inundated with messages across their entire lives; it takes a variety of impressions to make a message resonate with authenticity. So while one tactic might be your "most likely to succeed," using other tactics to support it makes good marketing sense.

Consider Dell and its online advertising and direct marketing programs. These efforts are the bread and butter of the United States' number two computer manufacturer.

Yet Dell also uses social media to garner customer feedback before a launch. It relies on initiatives like Idea Storm, and it seeds early interest in its products with blogger and customer reviews. Then after products launch, Dell uses social media to facilitate customer service.

Sequencing and Weaving

Good timing and sequencing blends old-fashioned marketing skills with communications *savoir-faire*, and building an initiative requires advance work to ensure maximum impact.

This is particularly true of time-limited initiatives—short marketing campaigns to drive holiday sales, or new product launches. Sequencing and weaving tactics together acknowledges that while you are relying on a primary tactic to promote a new product—say, public relations—other tactics will ease market adoption of the product.

In a hypothetical situation, say you use a public relations lead. You may want to galvanize and prepare your core team and most ardent supporters before you launch that PR campaign. Prelaunch buzz can only make a product more interesting and newsworthy.

You definitely want to prepare your friendly online influencers and select media outlets, if possible, before the launch. Your community of online advocates may enjoy being a part of the effort and see their roles as contributing to a larger initiative (and, hopefully, a successful one) for a brand they like.

Further, multichannel communications involves more than one tactic to achieve an objective. Maximum success is contingent upon working together to achieve larger objective. So in our hypothetical PR-led campaign, it also makes sense to consider direct marketing—mail or email—to inform loyal customers about a product as soon as it becomes available. Giving them the first opportunity to purchase the product is a way to strengthen your existing customer base.

In the movie *Up in the Air,* Ryan Bingham (George Clooney's character) said, "There's nothing cheap about loyalty." But new initiatives to reward your customers are well worth the effort.

Your marketing round is supporting the main PR effort with social media and direct marketing. But this is an important launch; there will be significant media stories and online conversations. Knowing that, it may make sense to support that buzz with some targeted advertising.

Consider how online advertising can bolster corporate social media efforts. A 2011 TNS Digital Life report showed that more than six in ten social media users admitted they are driven to engage with brands online by a promotion or special offer.

You can see how weaving comes into play, as well as sequencing the launch. Though PR is the lead, the effort starts with social, then moves into PR—which coincides with a short advertising burst and a direct marketing program to loyal customers. The multichannel effort, if executed well, is designed for maximum impact.

Visualizing the Comprehensive Multichannel Campaign

A multichannel approach is comprehensive in several ways, in medium and approach. When you weave, you overcome the weaknesses of one-directional approaches.

So using our PR example, instead of just having a top-down PR strategy, you also are going right to the middle with your direct marketing. Even better, your campaign is augmented with groundswell techniques (social) and flanking techniques (advertising).

When you envision the entire effort aimed toward achieving goals, you can sequence events accordingly. As the campaign moves through time, other tactics can be added—such as trade events and speaking engagements. Or as the news value of a product launch wanes, you could transition to the primary use of direct marketing and advertising.

Certainly, visualizing such a campaign gets complicated quickly. That's when it's time to take your calendar of events and plot out your campaign elements—put it all in one place so that you can see the whole timeline.

A simple, color-coded Excel sheet can go a long way toward helping you see the campaign as it will play out. Give each tactic its own color, and then use individual Excel sheet quadrants to place individual activities (see Figure 10.2).

Launch Calendar

Activity	October			
	1	8	15	22
Federal Holidays		X		
Industry Events				
Advertising	Creative development, one-time buy in *NY Times, USA Today*, online ad buy	Finalize creative, C. Day	Ads sent to papers, Facebook ads tested	Print ads run, social ads launched
Direct Marketing		C. Day	Write product x email	Email sent during launch event
PR	Finalize launch event details	Secure exclusive on product x	3Q Financial	Launch event, full-on media relations effort
Interactive/Social	Blogs on problems product x resolves, influencer relations, influencer outreach	Brief blogger advisory board, invite to launch event	Take ad creative, create Fbook iFrame, social ads, blog widget, custom landing pages for print ads, social activity	Live stream launch, embargo ends for blogs, ads, blog posts, ad widget, social ad: All systems go

Figure 10.2   *Sample launch calendar.*

This timed, multichannel approach applies to almost every sector. The calendar helps you manage with confidence as you move from planning to implementation, no matter what sector you are in.

When Atlas Corps won the Pepsi Refresh contest, it bolstered its email and social media efforts by building coalitions, as well as creating schedules of early outreach to its core online investors. Atlas replicated this success in fundraising contests like America's Giving Challenge and Chase.

Seizing the Lead

"Because you can win quickly by taking the lead, it is one of the most important things in strategy," said Musashi in his strategy classic *The Book of Five Rings.* Extending the concept to the modern era of competitive business, this is a timeless truth in marketing.

In the fall of 2011, Amazon and Kindle had an epic race to be first—the first to undercut Apple's iPad in the low-cost tablet market. Amazon was launching the Kindle Fire, and Barnes & Noble launched the Nook.

These companies did something that almost every other tablet manufacturer failed to do: They successfully competed with the iPad. But the keys to their success were things they had that other companies didn't. They had loyal customer bases, and they had existing products—the Kindle and Nook e-readers—that could be reformulated into content-agnostic tablets.

By galvanizing their core customers and existing content distribution mechanisms, Amazon and Barnes & Noble saw a clear path to leadership. The only thing in their way? Each other.

The horse race began with each company announcing next-generation tablets. Amazon positioned itself as a $199 alternative to the $500 entry-level iPad in a very Apple-esque launch announcement of the Kindle Fire in New York City in late September 2011. Barnes & Noble followed suit a month later, announcing that it was releasing an upgraded version of its color reader called the Nook Tablet. Priced at $250, the Tablet was a little costlier, and similarly styled as a reader's tablet.

The battle ensued to see which company would get its tablet to the market first. Both were aiming for Black Friday, and both companies beat expectations and got products into stores the week before Thanksgiving 2011. But because the timing of the two launches coincided within a week of each other, market factors weighed against Barnes & Noble.

Historically, in the reader marketplace, Barnes & Noble had not achieved market leadership because its product had slightly fewer features and was more costly. Further, Amazon already had the market-share lead with its prior generation of readers and has a much wider range of content at its disposal, including books, music, and video available through its Amazon Prime service.

When you have the lead, as Amazon did with its Kindle and Prime content products, it is difficult for competitors to unseat you. While the low-cost reader market leader is still being determined, the Kindle Fire leapt to an early market lead, with an estimated five million units sold by year-end 2011. B&N said it shipped one million Nook tablets by year end.

If Barnes & Noble had launched its consumer tablet six months before the Kindle Fire, it would have had a leg up on Amazon, making Amazon's climb to achieve first place a lot steeper.

As your marketing round evaluates when and how to launch products, it has to consider whether the competition is developing similar products or services. Then not only does multichannel marketing become important, but so does literally beating the competition to market to seize an early lead.

If word of mouth ensues, a leadership position can begin to develop. Marketing's role at that point is to communicate the leadership position, to trumpet why the product is superior, and to expand market share to a dominant position.

Adding Diagnostic Measurement to the Plan

Measurement has always been positioned as a benchmarking tool to prove results. Of course your marketing round wants to demonstrate results.

Yet in the midst of a campaign, measurement can show you what's working, what's not, and how the effort may play out. It can provide a diagnostic of your program in near real-time and allow you to adjust the program and make course corrections.

Nineteenth-century department store magnate John Wanamaker is credited with the legendary marketing joke "Half the money I spend on advertising is wasted; the trouble is, I don't know which half."

In today's marketing world, that's no longer true. The incorporation of unique URLs and strong measurement packages, from the free Google Analytics to robust enterprise services that companies such as Eloqua offer, enable you to determine customer behavior.

Web site measurement tools tell you what referred a person's visit to your site, when they visited, and what they did after they arrived—from length of visit to pages viewed. Calls to action allow your marketing round to convert those visits into real outcomes on the site, giving you additional measurement capabilities.

Whether your campaign is designed to brand and create awareness or to deliver sales or leads, there is no excuse for not keeping track. You need to measure.

Using the near-real-time availability of today's analytics software, you should be able to tell how a campaign is performing in the moment. That's all the more important in troubled economic times, when marketing success is key to many departments' existence. And for cause communicators, the ability to change course midstream based on real-time data and analysis can effect a different, better result from their communication efforts.

When you build, time, and sequence your campaign, you should consider how to integrate diagnostics. Use measurement benchmarks to determine the success of the overall effort, in addition to the performance of individual tactics.

Much of the dialogue around measurement deals with what to measure. People always want to pin a hard number on something like page views, retweets, or number of ad impressions. That's a good start, but does it tell you anything substantive?

Not likely. Success begins with changed perceptions or hard actions. This is where you have to add benchmarks that indicate whether your desired outcome is being achieved.

Is tonality changing in online conversations? What about a poll? Are people visiting the Web site? How do they find it? Are they identifying themselves with email addresses and requests for more information?

Good measurement involves qualitative benchmarks as well as quantitative ones. If your campaign is meant to elicit a certain result in a period of time—for example, 3,000 sales in three months—then you can create benchmarks. If you are relying on word of mouth to help sales, you could set a goal of 500 units in the first month, 1,000 in the second, and 1,500 in the third. These metrics can apply to just about any tactic.

A car-engine company may want to change perceptions of green cars by creating a more favorable impression of hydrogen-fueled cars versus fuel cells. Would you just measure hydrogen fuel posts? Or would you measure posts that mentioned both technologies, as well as the posts' tonality? You also would want to measure tonality at the start, as well as throughout the campaign, to determine progress, course corrections, and future direction.

There are many things a company can measure:

- Sales resulting from any of the marketing round's actions (use custom URLs and codes in calls to action to determine where traffic comes from)
- Number of attendees who decided to attend an event or a webinar
- Increased email list
- The development of self-identified community members who serve as an activism core online
- Changed brand perception
- Heightened awareness of the company (simply put, branding) as a thought leader
- Increased conversations on a topic (hydrogen engines, for example)

Don't let numbers such as Facebook "Likes," impressions, and Web site page views drive measurement. It's not enough to cite page views, unique visitors, or even the number of positive versus negative comments online. Analysis of the numbers in context with the original goals is crucial.

Exercises

Grounding your marketing roundtable's campaigns in a tactical plan begins with understanding the marketplace and the competitive field. Start a spreadsheet or an electronic calendar listing all pertinent items, including these:

- Federal holidays
- Industry events
- Any competitor events
- Internal events and initiatives

You may want to consider color-coding your various marketing disciplines, such as advertising, direct marketing, events, interactive, public relations, and social media. As you select tactics, you can add them to the calendar.

When you begin populating your calendar, start with your lead tactic. From there you can see how the marketing round can (or cannot) support the primary tactic. Add tactics to strengthen your effort's progress toward specific outcomes.

As you add tactics to the calendar, you can imagine how your customer will receive your communications—an integrated experience across channels. Vet the experience with your colleagues in the round and see how you can further support it.

While visualizing the campaign in the calendar, weigh the effort's customer reach and expected impact. Then add measurement levers to diagnose success. You could plan a weekly meeting to go over results and campaign health. From there, you can adjust and augment the campaign as needed.

11

Measure Results to Dollars and Cents

Given how much time and financial investment goes into building a successful marketing program, it only makes sense for organizations to measure and sustain critical outreach programs, online relationships, Web properties, and direct marketing initiatives. It also is the quickest way to determine whether a program is failing and adjust accordingly.

Ten years ago it would take a year or more to learn whether your campaigns were working. And it would take expensive brand-awareness studies, focus groups, and market research—a cost-prohibitive prospect for companies outside the Fortune 500. Today you can measure results daily, weekly, and monthly. You can adjust and refine immediately. Measurement is ultimately the answer to not only achieving success, but maintaining it.

You can't skip to the end and start measuring before you know what you need to measure, and that's why this topic is so far into this book. You need to build your marketing round, understand where the strengths of your team lie, really break down the silos (which is going to take some time), get your executives onboard, and discover which approaches and tactics you're going to use before you can implement a measurement program.

As you do all of those things, though, you can also begin to build your benchmarks and your dashboard. It will take 75 to 90 days to get it right, to understand what you should be measuring, and to know what the right goals are for the campaign, program, or year.

Your first benchmark may very well be zero. Or, perhaps you already have some things that are working really well and you want to not only integrate those efforts, but also grow them.

Take, for instance, Bill Prettyman, the CEO of WISE Printing. In 2010, he wanted to increase his personal brand within the industry. As incoming president of the Print Services & Distribution Association, he felt it was important that his peers, colleagues, and competitors in the print distribution industry know who he was before he took office.

He started, from scratch, a simple, blog-focused marketing program—benchmark: zero. His measurement was how many people approached him at conferences and networking events to mention his blog posts.

As he began his tenure as president of the trade organization, his goals were being met. People recognized his face, and they also grew familiar with his thinking and his philosophies because they read his blog. From there, he began to tie search, sales, and some additional brand awareness in to his goals.

Catalytic Products International, the maker of oxidizers, however, was focused on sales results when it began to implement a marketing round program in late 2010.

Using a combination of online advertising, trade shows, email marketing, content (white papers, educational newsletters, case studies), search engine optimization, media relations, search engine marketing, and a new Web site, it set out to test and benchmark results.

An oxidizer can be a multimillion-dollar purchase. Also, the sales cycle typically is 18 months through five years, depending on the type of company that is buying. The marketing round set out to shorten the sales cycle, while also showing a return, as it relates to revenue *and* profits.

In one year, the marketing round generated $2.2 million in new revenue, which was a return on investment of 8:1. As it compared the marketing round efforts to gross margins, it discovered a return on investment of 3:1, which created goodwill inside the organization toward the efforts.

As you can see, results mean different things to different business leaders. You can be sure, however, to always have success if you take an integrated approach like CPI. If you can demonstrate results to shortened sales cycles and increasing sales that lead to either higher margins or higher profits, the marketing round becomes an investment instead of an expense. However, if you focus solely on brand awareness and number of fans, followers, or readers, you will always be an expense—one that is easily cut when times get tough.

Create Benchmarks and Develop a Dashboard

There are many ways to measure results, especially in today's digital world. Gone are the days of media impressions and advertising equivalencies and Nielsen ratings and open rates. Today you should measure what each individual person does when the person interacts with your company, offline and on.

Some people will say they got into marketing because they're not good at numbers. The disciplines are very right-brained. But if the marketing round is going to succeed, you must channel your left brain to measure results.

According to a Forrester study,[1] the marketing round's role today is less and less about marketing and communication, and more and more about corporate strategy and leadership. This means the things you measure must be less and less engagement, influence, and sentiment, and more and more revenue, improved margins, and increased profits.

It's typical to measure one or two tactics as you learn how to benchmark and which data points to watch. Eventually you'll be able to measure strategy. Don't be fearful if it doesn't come immediately. Take the small wins and measure the results on one tactic as you get comfortable with the data, the metrics, and building your dashboard.

Your marketing round is going to be faced with a ton of data. And its job is to determine which metrics are valuable and which are not.

For instance, unique visitors, bounce rate, white paper downloads, and filling out a form to request more information may be the only things you need to consider. Or, total Web site visitors, email click-throughs, and shopping-cart abandonment rates may be all you need to consider. There definitely is not a one-size-fits-all approach.

Some of those tactical measurements will include your low-hanging fruit, such as the number of email addresses you have in your customer relationship management program, internal communication and sharing, sales pipeline, improvement in the sales cycle, growth in Web visitors, attendance at events, or online sites that require registration.

There are things that are important to business growth, such as brand awareness, sentiment, credibility, thought leadership, and even engagement and influence. But those things can't be completely tied to numbers. If you consider, however, *how* you achieve each of those things, you can measure their effectiveness.

Unless your Web site is antiquated, you need a few things to measure results. They include Google analytics, Clicky or Name Tag, the customer relationship management software (which could include Constant Contact, Salesforce, or Microsoft Dynamic), a monitoring service (such as Spiral16, Radian6, or Sysomos), and the content management system that hosts your Web site and/or blog.

Some of these tools are free. Others start at $59 and go up from there. You also can have what you measure automated through an API developed with your Web site and the other tools, but an easy way to get started is to develop a dashboard you manually update once a week.

Then you're going to develop the metrics to watch. For instance, if you're doing search engine marketing, you'll want to consider click-through rate, average position, quality score, impression share, bounce rate, and conversion rate. The click-through and bounce rates will tell you whether the program is working. Are people not clicking, so that rate is really low? Or are people clicking on your Google AdWord, coming to your landing page, and then leaving immediately, driving a high bounce rate (higher than 50 percent)? Neither of those necessarily means search engine marketing isn't working, but perhaps you need to do some serious revisions to your ads and landing pages to try to increase your click-through rate and reduce your bounce rate.

As you build your dashboard, create your metrics, and analyze the weekly results, be sure you understand how each company (Google, Clicky, CRM, monitoring) analyzes its numbers. And do some research to discover the industry standards. For instance, a bounce rate of less than 40 percent is excellent for any industry. You can find industry averages for nearly every metric with a simple Google search.

In the "Exercises" section at the end of this chapter, you will build your dashboard report. Get your CFO involved. Get sales involved. Work with them to figure out which metrics are the right ones to measure. For instance, you may discover it takes 1,000 total visitors and 800 unique visitors to generate one request for a quote. And the marketing round converts every fourth request for a quote to one customer. So your goal for each customer equals 4,000 visitors and 3,200 unique visitors.

You will continue building your dashboard based on the benchmarks and information you already have. You'll adjust and make changes as you begin measuring strategy instead of tactics. That will come with time.

Making Decisions

At some point you will have to let a program go because it's not generating the results you expected. The good news is, with the dashboard you've so carefully built, and with the weekly reporting you're doing with the marketing round to the executive team, you'll find out pretty quickly which program to ditch.

For instance, it can take all of an hour to discover the keywords you've labored over for your pay-per-click campaign to drive white paper downloads is much too expensive and you ran out of budget on the first click.

Or you'll discover curating content for your email marketing isn't getting any click-throughs or has more than two percent unsubscribes.

Whatever it happens to be, making the decision to cut the program, revise the thinking, or invest more money should happen every week during your marketing round meetings.

If the metrics show something isn't working, stop doing it. If it isn't tied to revenue, improved margins, or increased profits, stop doing it. Watch the running totals week after week and month after month and, if they're not increasing, stop doing it.

If you can prove a return on investment like Catalytic Products International did in 2011, it won't be hard to invest more in marketing. That's always the goal. Show a real return on your efforts that translate into more money for the company, and your marketing round will be rewarded with additional budget. And you will reap the benefits of success.

Exercises

Develop the Benchmarks

To determine the right things to measure and build your dashboard, consider the following questions:

- What types of campaigns will be tracked? Are you tracking leads, cultivating those leads, converting those leads, or all of the above? Know exactly what you need to track to be successful.
- How do cross-channel communication and campaigns roll into a single program?
- What information is available to match a customer response, and how will you track that response through the process?
- How will all of the data be managed? Will each person in the marketing round be responsible for a portion of the dashboard, or will you have one analytics person reporting during the weekly meetings? If it's the latter, education for each discipline around analytics must be ongoing.

The metrics you develop should include sales, lead generation, lead nurturing, lead conversion, thought leadership, Web traffic, and brand awareness. In this exercise, create a goal for each of those seven categories, and, for the next 90 days, see what kind of effect the marketing round efforts have on the business. These will become your benchmarks that you'll report on as you grow the marketing round.

Build the Dashboard

Now it's time to build the dashboard. Based on the benchmarks you've created, you're going to find some trends.

For instance, if your goal is to provide a webinar series to generate leads, you can begin to work backward. How many people must attend one free webinar to generate enough leads to convert one customer? The number will vary, based on your industry and price point, but the data you're collecting through Google, Clicky or Name Tag, your customer relationship management software, and the monitoring program will give you enough information to figure this out.

If you don't sell product online, but want people to submit a request for more information, you can work backward to determine how many Web visits, unique visits, and Google ad click-throughs, as well as what kind of bounce rate, it takes to get one request.

As you determine these goals, you'll want to include them at the top of your dashboard (see Figure 11.1) and then track against them every month, with a running total to guide your decisions.

Month	Web Visits	Unique Visits	Request a Quote	Request for Information	Contact Requests	WP Downloads	Newsletter Clicks	Leads Generated	Leads Converted	Revenue	Profit
Goals											
January											
February											
March											
April											
May											
June											
July											
August											
September											
October											
November											
December											

Figure 11.1   *An example of a dashboard you'll build to measure your results.*

Endnote

1.   www.forrester.com/imagesV2/uplmisc/The_EvolvedCMO.pdf.

12

Respect and Anticipate Community and Competition

Experienced strategists know that migration—the drift of customers to new and different forms of media—is normal. The trajectory so far has started with print media and tacked to radio to television to cable to the Internet to mobile.

People move from media platform to media platform, seeking experiences that offer good information, entertainment, ease of use, and the best overall value in their day-to-day lives. Your marketing round has to move with them.

That mobility means a greater likelihood of success— which your competition will react to by adapting its approach to challenge yours. And so it goes.

In marketing, no approach is certain. What is certain is that we all are working within a dramatically changing media landscape that has moved faster with each new decade.

When the digital revolution was fomented in the 1990s by Tim Berners-Lee, Marc Andreessen, and the group of programmers who created Internet technologies like Mosaic and the Netscape browser, the World Wide Web era was born. The pace of change accelerated, and social and mobile media have only sped things further—instead of new media developing every decade or so, marketers are confronted with new tools and uses of media at every turn, sometimes multiple new avenues in a single year.

In 2011, Google+ and Instagram—two very successful social networks—were launched. And Instagram is completely mobile.

In broadcasting, the explosion of online conversational media unleashed the beginnings of the Social TV revolution. This is pushing broadcasters and marketers to create content that works beyond the TV program and the 30-second ad spot.

Change is your marketing round's constant. Evolution—via Kindle Fires, Apple TVs, or iPhone apps—is inevitable. You have to evaluate and decide how much effort you dedicate to traditional media, and how much you commit to the new digital and mobile venues.

Measurement as a Diagnostic

One great aspect of a measurement program is the window it gives your marketing round into stakeholder activity. Although there will be unexplainable, temporary shifts, measurement programs can show, overall, when stakeholders are changing their media use and behavior.

Discussing those behavior changes as a regular part of your marketing round conversation makes sense. For example, armed with that information, your advertising and social media teams can together make a progressive decision on how to approach Social TV.

To effectively monitor your stakeholders' media use, we recommend building a dashboard that measures traffic sources and events on your Web site. Here are some tips to get started:

- Use your web analytics package to measure sources of traffic.
- Make it stakeholder-specific.
- If necessary or possible, break into specific stakeholder groups using URLs and social media accounts, and custom content.

- Match traffic spikes against events. Did a new ad campaign
  launch? Was there a significant media story or a major blog
  post? Was a direct marketing campaign launched?
- What keywords are people using to find your site?
- Use consistent measures to benchmark performance over time.

You can keep the dashboard data in as simple a format as an Excel file,
and then extrapolate the data in charts and graphs from week to week (or
however frequently you meet). Use the charts to visually lay out data and
inform your marketing round.

Within a multichannel marketing effort, you will see cross-pollination of
traffic across media. But you will also see shifts in behavior. For example,
the effect of media announcements may wane in comparison to other
efforts. This is a clear signal to migrate your method of communicating
news, perhaps to a blog or other means.

Additionally, if you have an active social media effort that is truly engaged
with your community, you should be able to see when new media are rising. For example, if Social TV is a new phrase for you, then you are likely
not active online. It has been a growing trend throughout 2011 and moving
forward, with 86 percent of U.S. adults who have smartphones using them
to comment online while watching TV (source: Yahoo!).

While stakeholder behavior can clearly demarcate emerging media trends,
it also may indicate that your customers' media use is static. Even then,
your marketing round should experiment with new media and innovative
efforts within exiting outreach channels. Market leadership is rarely developed by following the pack.

For example, almost all of our experiences show that when a company or
nonprofit makes their site mobile-friendly, they seek dramatic increases in
mobile traffic. Often they see Web traffic numbers rapidly rising in the 10
percent range by simply catering to Web-based smartphones and tablets.
This jump in mobile traffic is without adding applications or location-
based social network services.

Be open to innovation with new media—even setting aside a single percentage of your budget for experimentation allows you the flexibility to try new
things.

When the Customer Rises

Most marketers are afraid of social media–driven virtual riots; no one wants a pack of raving bloggers attacking their brand in a flurry of peer-driven angst.

Although there is a kernel of truth to the "crazy bloggers" scenario, these incidents usually are caused by upset customers. Even the strongest marketing campaigns and most-famous brands are not immune to customer angst. And the traditional press still plays a role in outing companies.

The Amazon Kindle Fire launched with great success during the 2011–12 holiday season; sales outpaced Amazon's forecast of five million units. But the iPad competitor had quality issues; more than 30 percent of buyers rated the device "negative to neutral (1 to 3 stars)."

The *New York Times* ran an extensive piece about the Fire's foibles. As Amazon forged ahead with its less-than-perfect Fire, negative reviews piled up. And more media reported about them. When you see the product on Amazon, it is listed as a 4-star product, not at all representative of the significant minority of dissatisfaction.

Negative reviews were left unanswered by Amazon's customer service team, which is a common practice among corporate brands. The company took a software product attitude of "we'll fix it later or as we go," but did not apologize. A promise to fix problems through software updates was their only action.

Though Amazon has a lot of brand loyalty to trade upon, in the long term such a slow response is unlikely to thwart a negative customer undercurrent.

If the marketing strategy for the Kindle Fire is all about ubiquity through low-cost sales, then the fastest way to ensure success is not just to sell a lot of them, but to quickly address customer service issues to inspire positive word-of-mouth marketing.

Addressing such issues means showing respect for your marketing round's customers, even those who have had a negative experience. Not responding to those who complain, or denying that their complaints are valid, is the fastest path to negative word of mouth.

These groundswells of angst often find their way online and damage your brand's reputation. But they're not the only source of crisis. The media is quite capable of creating a crisis moment for your brand.

Consider what happened to Toyota when it blamed unrestrained acceleration issues on the floor mats in its vehicles. Within three months of widely publicized fatalities involving Toyota accelerators, the *Los Angeles Times* reported on October 18, 2009, that there had been nine National Highway Traffic Safety Administration investigations into Toyota accelerator incidents and that hundreds of complaints had been filed with the agency. Five of the investigations included fatalities, and six involved unproven phantom accelerator incidents. Only two of the nine incidents were definitively caused by floor mats.

And it got worse for Toyota. The company sent a letter to all its customers advising of a coming recall to address the acceleration issue, yet denying any automobile defect. This prompted an extremely unusual public rebuke from NHTSA—the safety agency said there was, indeed, a defect.

Toyota continued denying the problem, which triggered further investigations, including another *Los Angeles Times* article that revealed 1,200 acceleration complaints had been filed with NHTSA. On December 26, 2009, another accident occurred with a Toyota Avalon. Four people died. Its floor mats were in the trunk.

Over the next month, Toyota announced a series of escalating recalls for 7.5 million vehicles in the United States, and the Department of Transportation asked the company to stop selling these vehicles until they were fixed. The crisis is estimated to have cost Toyota and its dealers more than $4 billion in revenue and 10 percent of its stock value during the week of the recalls. Once a beloved brand, Toyota was viewed unfavorably by 29 percent of Americans after the incident, according to February 2010 market research by the firm Rasmussen.

The irony of this horribly handled crisis was that the media, and Toyota's continuing denials of customer, media, and government complaints, fanned it.

All the dramatic financial losses, reputation issues, and possibly some fatalities could have been avoided if Toyota had simply addressed its customer complaints promptly—especially given that *Car and Driver* and *Consumer*

Reports issued stories in February 2010 showing that Toyota cars, even with the defects, were 20 times less likely to produce a fatal accident than other automobiles.

If multiple customers complain about a single issue, listen. Repetition is a red flag. At a minimum, you should acknowledge the customers and thank them for their feedback.

And don't sit on that customer feedback. In today's world, it's likely that your department and the customer service department will both hear from customers. So work together on who delivers the response and what it should be. If the customers get two responses, especially if they're different, they'll wonder who's minding the store.

This is not just for the betterment of your public relations effort, but to preserve your brand's integrity. In the end, your brand value is the result of your marketing round's efforts and the quality of your company's product.

Respect Your Competitors

Marketing extends beyond stakeholders and organizations. Although companies like to pretend that they operate alone in their industries, competition exists—even if all the competitors are wrestling for is stakeholders' time and money.

If marketers do their job well, and their product, service, or solution gets a warm reception, the competition won't sit and watch while your marketing round takes away market share. They will act.

Here are five competitive responses you can expect:

1. **Pretend You Don't Exist**

    This is the most short-sighted and foolish response. The ostrich approach fools no one. Customers know there are alternatives, and so do the media and bloggers.

    When a company acts as though it exists in an industry vacuum, it looks like it's posturing or gunning for transactions. Consumers expect this, so the company's communications are perceived as completely brand-related, and customers are less willing to trust it.

It's hard for a company to develop industry leadership when it doesn't acknowledge the reality of its marketplace, even in a general way. Apple rarely talks about HP or Dell, specifically, but it certainly acknowledges and talks about other PCs and smartphones. Car companies discuss industry accolades, which is smart, because it puts their product within a competitive context. Such acknowledgment is authentic, and it inspires trust.

2. **Mimic Your Offering**

When a company does really well, a common competitive response is to offer the same product or service: After Amazon launched the Kindle, Barnes & Noble offered the Nook. When Cirque du Soleil's artistic acrobatics revolutionized big-top entertainment, other circuses added Cirque-like elements to their shows.

It's always good to have an established market share when a competitor mimics your offering, because then your company has the lead. But the competition's efforts still can be quite disconcerting. There have been instances when a company like Netflix or Google rises up and wrests the market away from a Blockbuster or Yahoo! but this is usually through some sort of technological innovation.

The key is to not overreact to the competition. Continue innovating on the product or service offering and work to extend your lead in the marketplace. Don't rest on your laurels.

3. **Trash, Sue, and Undercut**

Apple is suing Google, claiming the search giant copied the iPhone iOS with its Android phones. As part of a strategy to strengthen its case, Google recently purchased Motorola Mobility to acquire its patents.

Other common competitive acts include disparaging the competition publicly and privately, stealing talent through hiring of employees and contract firms, blocking product distribution, and undercutting pricing to seize market share.

These are the hard tactics of war in the market, and you have to be able to defend against them. You don't have to directly engage your competitor, but you do have to respond to your customers by giving them value and encouraging their loyalty.

That's the high road, and if it's at all possible, it's the road you should take. Trash talk, lawsuits, and price slashing are signs of truly contentious rivalry; they almost always make the market harder to work within, and they can reduce customer trust sectorwide. That doesn't grow the general market in any obvious way.

4. Go Toe-to-Toe

In an established market like car insurance, where offerings are very similar from company to company, it is not uncommon to see advertising that directly pits a company against its competitors. This is a common tactic. Sprint also uses it against Verizon and AT&T with its data and service plans.

There's not much you can do in that situation other than to clearly state why your product is better, and to engage in customer service and loyalty programs. This is about keeping customers by bettering their total experience—again, inspiring loyalty.

In the competitive wireless market, Sprint is currently a distant third, a gap that has increased over the past decade in large part because of the customer service issues the company experienced after acquiring Nextel. Having resolved many of these issues, it is now struggling to rebuild that market share.

5. Leapfrog Your Offering

The best response consists of a competitive product or service that is of significantly higher quality and/or more cost-effective or easier to use than yours. Although you might have the higher ground, this type of new offering creates green fields for your competitors. Customers flock to them.

Consider how Japanese companies beat their U.S. counterparts
in the electronics and automotive sectors in the '70s and '80s by
offering higher-quality products for lower costs. The result was
an incredible loss of market share and reputation for the U.S.
companies.

In this instance, speed is crucial. Loyal customers will stick with
you, but only if you are able to match or better the competitor's
offer quickly. Unfortunately, when faced with such a challenge,
most companies stick to doing business as usual. And thus new
brands seize market leadership.

When to Respond to the Competition

It has been a while since we've cited our Japanese sage, 17th-century
Japanese samurai Miyamoto Musashi. Here's what Musashi had to say
about competitors from his time: "If you fix your eyes on details and
neglect important things, your spirit will become bewildered, and victory
will escape you."

A significant percentage of executives find out about a competitor's move
only when it is announced.[1] That can send a company's marketing round
into an unfocused tizzy of overreaction and distract it from its most
important focus: customers.

There's big danger in overresponding to the competition, in focusing on
secondary and urgent-feeling goals instead of on the primary objective.
Those smaller issues become distractions, and distractions are a hindrance
to achieving success.

Your marketing round needs to know when to respond to a competitor's
actions. The scenarios that are most likely to require a response are a new
competitive offering or a price cut. In other instances, it's difficult to know
whether working to counteract a competitor is worth the investment or is
just a distraction.

Here are some questions to consider:

- Does the competitive response significantly increase the quality
  of their offering?
- Does it surpass your company's effort?

- Are you losing customers as a result of the competitive action?
- Are customers actively discussing your competitor on social media?
- Is the competitor getting fleeting attention from the media, or is there sustained marketplace buzz?
- Has the announcement hurt your brand equity?

If you are answering yes to some or all of these questions, you will want to respond. But respond intelligently. Think it through. Fifty-five percent of companies respond with the most obvious action, says McKinsey and Company. You want your response to yield a competitive advantage, not just noise.

Make sure the effort improves your offering to customers and the industry as a whole. Does it improve your product, increase customer loyalty, or demonstrate a quality commitment to the marketplace?

If necessary, your marketing round should work with the larger executive team to innovate your product or service before addressing the masses. A response that makes your company's product or service better is much more likely to succeed than a response for the sake of a response.

You will want to act with speed. Almost half of competitors wait at least six months to respond, and that can be dangerous. Research in Motion took more than a year to respond to the innovations that Apple's iPhone and Google's Android operating systems presented. The Blackberry operating system and phones were never able to catch up, and the company lost its place as the leading manufacturer of smartphones. Many pundits question whether Blackberries will be on the market by 2015.

If your answers to the previously listed competitive tests are primarily "no," it may be best to simply wish the competition well. Knowing when not to engage is part of a strategist's job.

Turning the other cheek when a competitor acts in a flashy manner can be one of the hardest acts of all for a marketing round. Yet building constant value and enhancing loyalty for your customers, and not responding to knockoffs and tired tactics, are what make your marketing substantially better than that of the competition.

Staying Sharp

Success is a fantastic thing. It makes you feel like the best, and, for a time, you are the best in your field. You and your marketing round proved that you were hungry enough to get there.

Similarly, failure can be powerful. When your company doesn't become successful over time, it can be easy to accept mediocrity.

As you can see from the discussion about customers and competition, the biggest dangers from a changing market are not that needs are ignored or the competition beats you. Rather, it is your company's (and your marketing round's) inability or unwillingness to adapt.

Maybe there's an executive-team failure. Or there are not effective monitoring processes, of both customers and competitors. Or the team thinks that the upset customers will go away and that their competitors are wrong. And sometimes companies rest on their laurels—thinking their earlier successes are enough to keep them competitive and on top.

These all-too-common attitudes are dangerous. Losing one's edge is a failing that dates to the ancient civilization that coined the "don't rest on your laurels" phrase. Wreaths of laurel leaves (similar to bay leaves) were given to champions in the original Olympic games.

Today, companies that become satisfied with their current level of success, or that cannot continue to innovate and serve their market intelligently, risk failure. Without hustle and a continued commitment to excellence, marketing and business initiatives can fall by the wayside.

"Hustle," as a work ethic, has been around for a long time. Pete Rose has to be considered the epitome of hustling (though his other ethics are certainly questionable). In more recent times people like Facebook's Mark Zuckerberg and Gary Vaynerchuk of WineLibrary TV fame have demonstrated that consistently dedicated work ethics—hustle—can lead to positive results.

When you hustle, your marketing round executes every initiative, small or large, as though it can give you a competitive advantage. You never give up, never assume you've won.

We are in a fractured, highly competitive media environment. New distribution and communication methods are developed every year. If you don't provide your stakeholders with a comprehensive brand experience and ways to engage your company, others will.

Competitive advantage demands hustle and a long-term commitment to creating compelling marketing for the company and its stakeholders. In an era when challenges can arise from so many different places, working with your marketing round as a team with a shared commitment to excellence is the best way to stay sharp.

Together you can anticipate and respond to customer issues and competitive actions with an eye toward continuing innovation and customer loyalty. Your company can keep its edge and stay ahead by continuing to build. Keep your eyes forward and never stop driving.

Exercises

Media Behavior Dashboard

Creating a dashboard using Microsoft Excel is easy, and it's a great way to report visualized data points to your marketing round. You can export data out of your Google Analytics package manually, or you can use a free Web-based plug-in like Excellent Analytics to import data into an Excel sheet.

The first thing to do is to qualify what data points you will measure. You should seriously consider using different landing pages for different demographics and media so you can measure their performance. Consider the following basic data points:

- Traffic sources (includes social and search)
- Mobile traffic
- Landing-page traffic
- Keyword searches

Use clearly delineated named ranges for columns. For example, "Social Sources: Facebook, Twitter, and Google+" is better than "G, H, and I." If you are an Excel wizard, you can create dynamic ranges, which allow you to add columns within a data range without messing up the entire sheet.

From there you can build macros to simplify addition, and most important, you can easily build simple charts, particularly with Microsoft Excel 2007 and 2010. If you are having a hard time with making charts from data for your dashboard, you can visit the Data Visualization Blog at www.excelcharts.com/blog/posts. It is full of excellent suggestions.

With your dashboard of data points, look for spikes and dips in the data and compare it to your calendar of marketing events for the round. You should see some correlation. Note any coinciding data points to help the marketing round's analysis of the dashboard. Epiphanies are not always obvious. Help the team see the connection.

Your marketing round will certainly have other sources for changing media, from social media buzz to news reports to firsthand experience. But the dashboard allows you to see customer behavior as it unfolds over time. Keep a history of reports so you can reference them.

Monitoring Competition

According to the McKinsey report "How Companies Respond to Competitors," only 23 percent of companies learn about a competitive innovation and only 12 percent learn of a pricing change in time to respond to it before an announcement. Worse, 48 percent hear about an innovation and 64 percent hear about a pricing change from the announcement itself or later.

This is in large part because news reports are a primary source of information for competitive data. To bolster your marketing round's ability to better respond to competitors, consider adding some of the following sources of additional competitive data:

- Annual reports and SEC filings
- Intelligence from industry groups, forums, and conferences
- Speeches from competitors' leaders
- Industry analyst reports
- Market research via consumer focus groups, interviews, and surveys

To help maintain this data, you may want to keep an internal, shared file that details your competitors' actions, marketing initiatives, intelligence, and rumors so you can refer to it.

Endnote

1. Kevin Coyne and John Horn, "How Companies Respond to Competitors: A McKinsey Global Survey," *McKinsey Quarterly*, May 2008, https://www.mckinseyquarterly.com/Strategy/Strategic_Thinking/How_companies_respond_to_competitors_2146.

Index

MARKETING
IN THE ROUND
How to Develop an Integrated
Marketing Campaign in the Digital Era

MULTICHANNEL
MARKETING

GINI DIETRICH & GEOFF LIVINGSTON

FREE
Online Edition

Safari
Books Online

Your purchase of *Marketing in the Round* includes access to a free online edition for 45 days through the **Safari Books Online** subscription service. Nearly every Que book is available online through **Safari Books Online**, along with thousands of books and videos from publishers such as Addison-Wesley Professional, Cisco Press, Exam Cram, IBM Press, O'Reilly Media, Prentice Hall, and Sams.

Safari Books Online is a digital library providing searchable, on-demand access to thousands of technology, digital media, and professional development books and videos from leading publishers. With one monthly or yearly subscription price, you get unlimited access to learning tools and information on topics including mobile app and software development, tips and tricks on using your favorite gadgets, networking, project management, graphic design, and much more.

Activate your FREE Online Edition at
informit.com/safarifree

STEP 1:   Enter the coupon code: BBARWBI.

STEP 2:   New Safari users, complete the brief registration form.
Safari subscribers, just log in.

If you have difficulty registering on Safari or accessing the online edition,
please e-mail customer-service@safaribooksonline.com

✗ Direct Marketing   for young people

one-on-one communication w/ customer
- printed piece → must have a social/fun component
- email   emailing programs.
                                     video and audio content
(page measurement with special links)

- social media - list built by opting in.
  branding, conversation, word of mouth
              time consuming - hard to measure sales
                              more popular
- Mobile
  smartphones + tablets + iphones
  short, visual,
  SMS (textings, which can be opted in/out
  Traffic-based -   (QR code)
  using applications.
  so → empower users as they choose applications
  The customer must opt in before marketing can
  engage -

Ask PEN # of people on each media -
  survey → prefered method of contact